ISSUE 03

Berkeley Arts + Design

Griffith Moon

Printed in the United States of America
First Printing, 2019

Published by Griffith Moon
Santa Monica, California
GriffithMoon.com

ISBN 978-1-7326992-3-6
Library of Congress Control Number: 2018938759

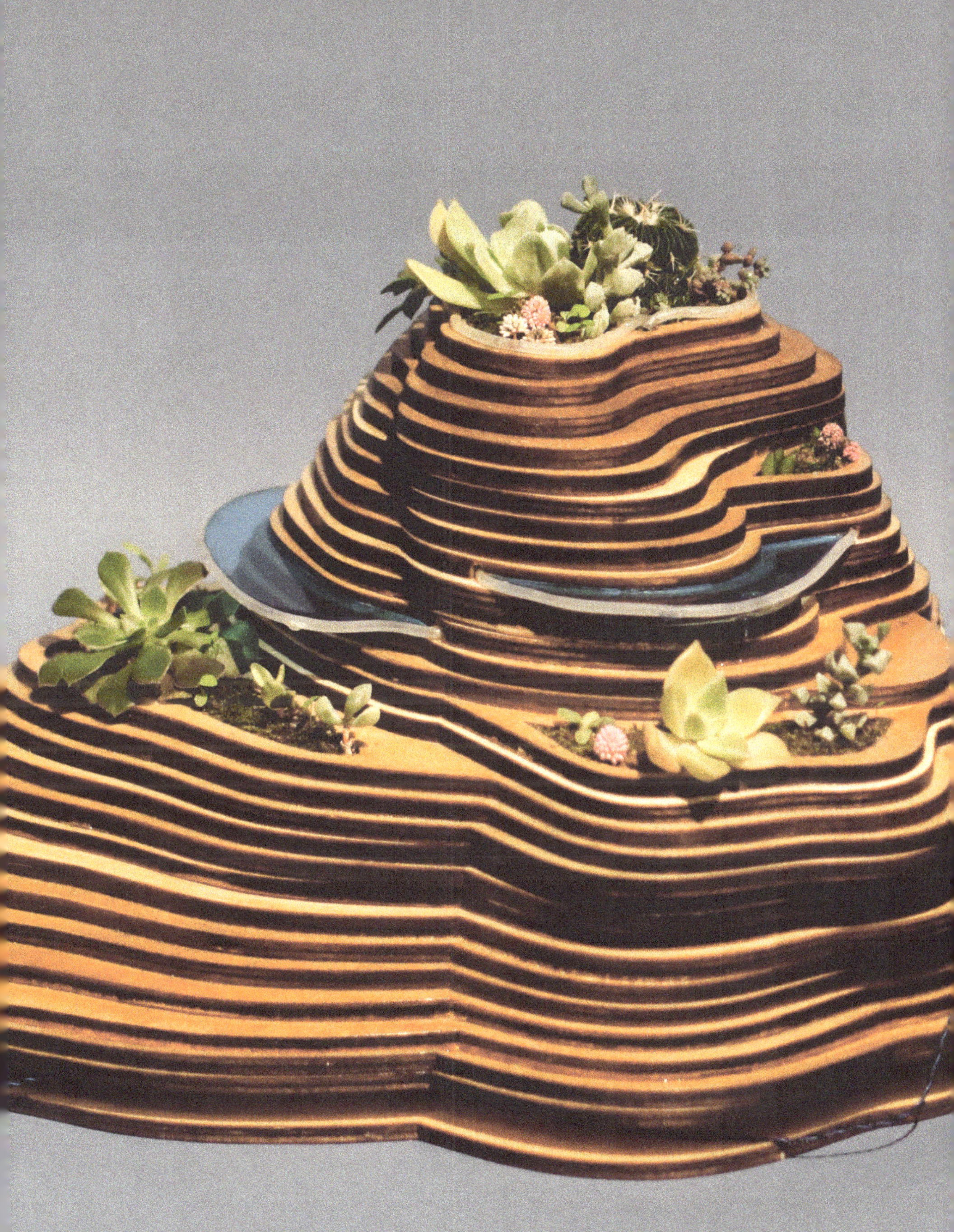

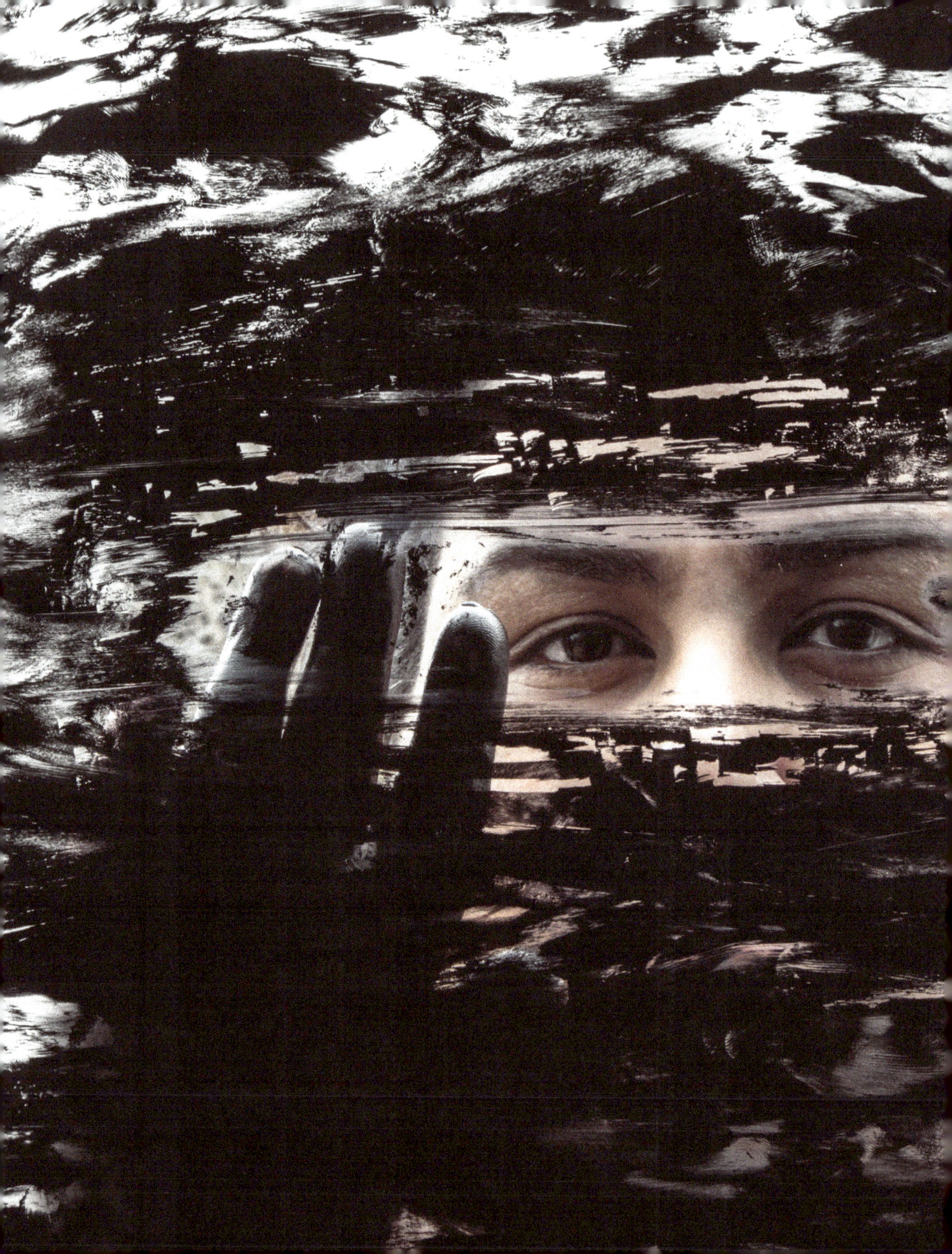

TABLE OF CONTENTS

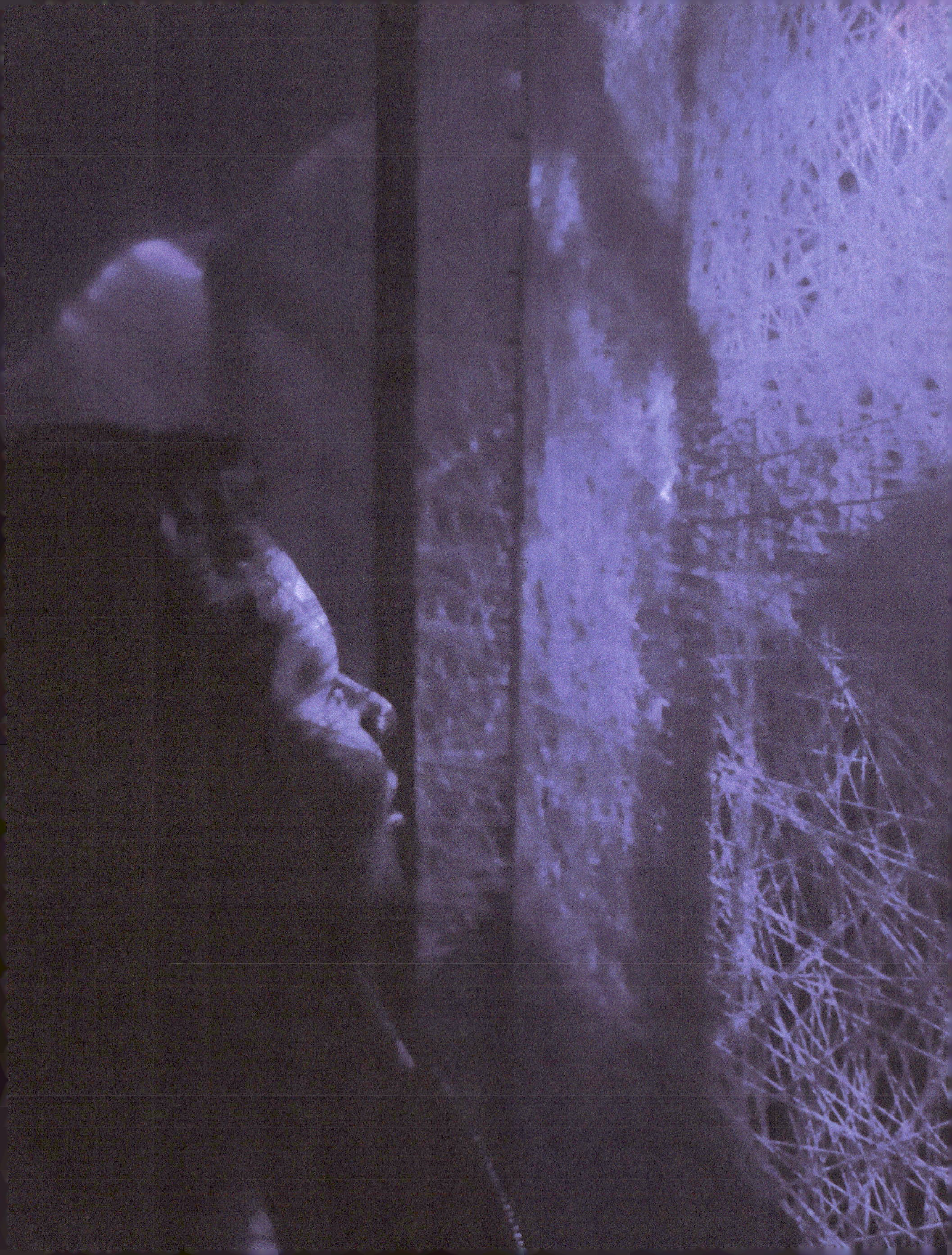

In 2018, we at Berkeley celebrated our sesquicentennial, and it has been a chance to take stock of a rich history of creative innovation and public impact. As the flagship campus of the University of California, Berkeley is one of the oldest educational institutions and also one of the oldest public institutions in the state. From its early commitments to poetry, architecture, music, and the 'practical arts,' the arts and design have been central to this deep and expansive legacy. Berkeley is a place of tradition and of innovation, a place of learning and place of transformative public dialogue. Creativity is essential to the history and to the future of our university; it is also essential to the future of California and to the future of our globally-connected world.

This book is the third in a series that seeks to represent the next stage of Berkeley's creative legacy. We gather outstanding work from across our undergraduate student population, representing a wide range of disciplines in performance, design, media, visual, and literary forms. The projects were nominated by our faculty and cover the entire creative spectrum—and then some! You will find group projects and solo pieces from departments such as English, Theater, Dance, and Performance Studies, and Art Practice as well as some from unexpected places—Computer Science, Mechanical Engineering, and Molecular Biology. Each year, we uncover hidden pockets of remarkable innovation, reminding us what it means to promote creativity at a public research university. We feel privileged, time and time again, to tap into these resources and share them with you.

Of course, the breadth of projects does not come as a surprise to those of us familiar with all that is *Made @ Berkeley*. With its wide-ranging interdisciplinary landscape of making and thinking, Berkeley stands out as a uniquely bracing context for creative experimentation: one enriched by the scientific and cultural wealth of a world-class research university; one propelled by our historic commitment to public access and social impact. Many of the projects assembled here speak to both of those potent strands: they both reimagine classic forms and create new, cross-disciplinary projects and real-world interventions. Moreover, it certainly is not surprising that so many of our creative students are preoccupied with pressing social issues and provide a model for how we can leverage creativity for the greater good.

Indeed, we have been struck by how many honored projects advance the signature goals of Berkeley's research culture. You will find here creative work that addresses issues of Environment and Climate, especially how climate change and the pursuit of sustainable future re-shapes contemporary ideas of human-nature interactions. You will also find Creative Discovery projects that ponder, rigorously and imaginatively, the role of the arts in supporting and communicating the future of Health and Wellness for individuals and society. Meanwhile, so much of Berkeley's creative landscape advances and exemplifies the goals of S.T.E.A.M., joining the arts with science and engineering to speculate on the future of intelligence, the impact of data, and the horizon of the virtual. We have organized the book with such Themes in mind—as well as others that you will find highlighted on the A+D website—as they propel research and inquiry on our campus. We have included a section on Cities, given the keen interest of our students in questions of urban experience and gentrification, as well as sections on Aesthetics and Fabrication that focus expressly on the manipulation of form, in text, image, gesture, space, and more. Finally, because so many of our students clearly position their work in a conversation with the challenges of democracy and inequality, you will find sections focused expressly issues of Gender and Sexuality, on the experience of Spirituality and transformation, and on the formation of Global Cultures in migratory world.

While these pages preserve some of the achievements of the past year, they are also meant as an invitation to you. At the end, we include two projects—both functional and speculative—sponsored by Berkeley Arts + Design: a new Arts Passport providing mobile arts access to students, thanks to engineering students at the Fung Institute, and an imaginative exploration of our historic home in the Dwinelle Annex, thanks to students in Professor Walter Hood's studio class. We hope that all of these works reveal and inspire. Such Creative Discovery projects are a reminder of what the "+" means for those of us in the Office of Berkeley Arts + Design. As we wrap up the year and look forward to more, we urge you to explore and connect with this incredible creative landscape.

Enjoy. Relish. Cherish.
Fiat Lux and Go Bears,

Shannon Jackson
Associate Vice Chancellor for the Arts and Design
University of California, Berkeley

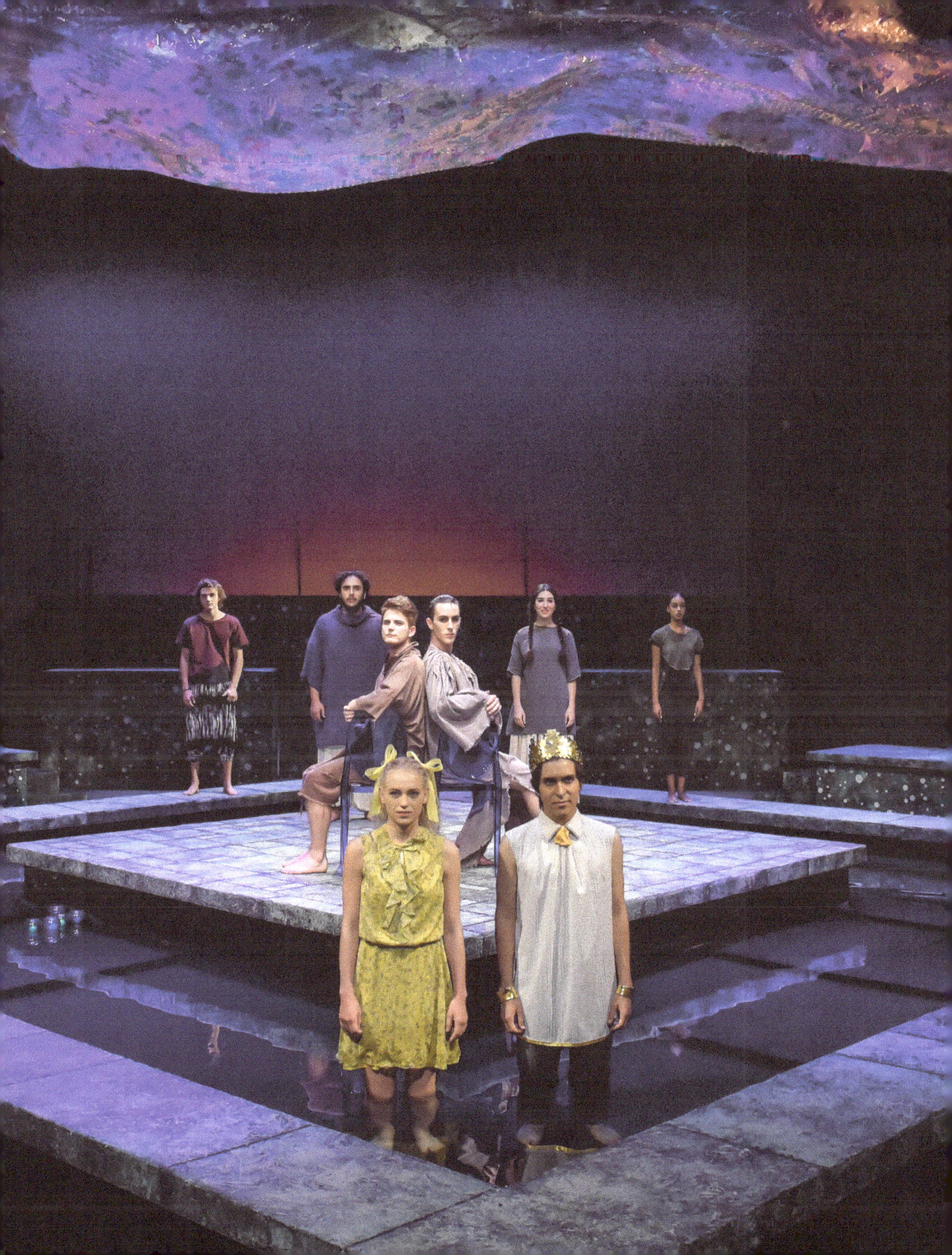

AESTHETICS

BOBBY GE

BRENNAN MCGEE

CADE JOHNSON

MARGARET CASTRO

NINA DJUKIC

SHREY MENDIRATTA

YAXUAN (JADEN) CHEN

Bobby Ge

Cascade is an orchestral work dedicated to the UC Berkeley Symphony Orchestra. Despite its relative brevity, the piece is symphonic in its emotional scale, seeking to explore the outermost limits of diatonicism over the course of its 10 minutes. It is a work of vast contrast, veering between arrhythmic masses of drifting pantonal clusters and firmly beat, atonal polyphony.

Bobby Ge (b. 1996) has composed orchestral and instrumental music since ninth grade. His music possesses a strongly dramatic character stemming from his love for film, and is influenced by strains of post-minimalism, late Romanticism, and elements of high modernity. Ge has served as the President of UC Berkeley's Undergraduate Composers Club for the last two years and is an Honors candidate in composition under music department chair Cindy Cox. He has also studied with Professors Robert Yamasato, Jean Ahn, and Franck Bedrossian. Ge begins his doctoral studies in composition at the Peabody Conservatory at Johns Hopkins this fall.

Bobby Ge
B.A. Music and Physics, 2018

Faculty Mentor: Cindy Cox, Music

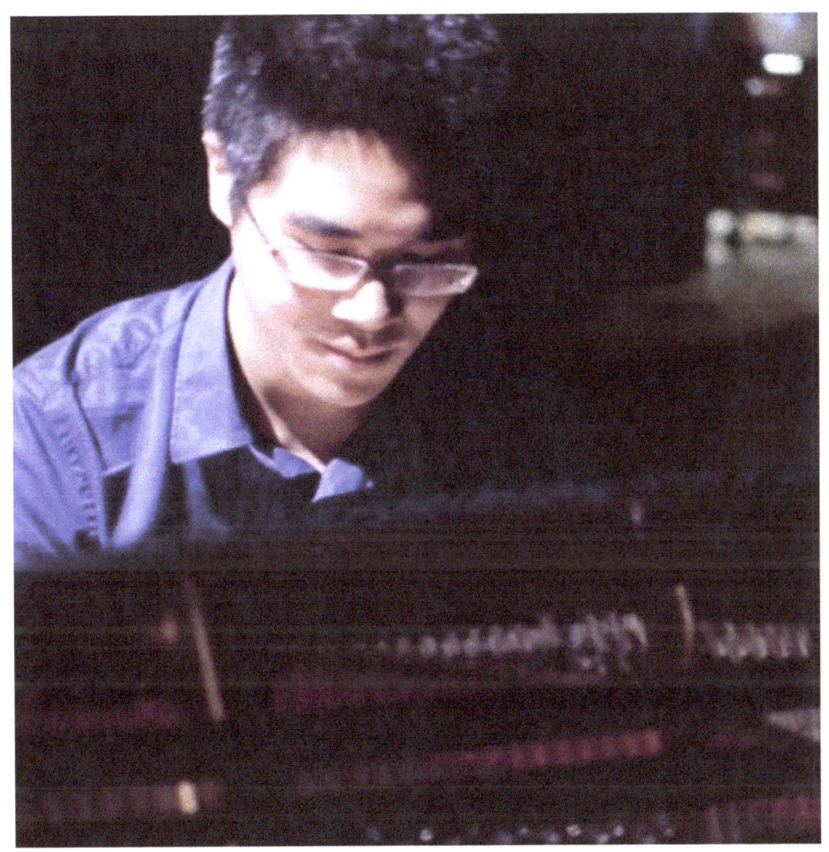

Cascade, for Symphony Orchestra, 2018. Symphony orchestra, 10:44 minutes.

Brennan McGee

In Apartment 28, a self-repressed filmmaker, Robbie, begins to embrace his identity following rejection by the girl of his dreams. Although the vision for this piece was my own, the collaboration from cast and crew alike is what made this piece what it is. Sunce Franicevic, the director of photography, was heavily involved on both aesthetic and narrative levels and was absolutely essential in the translation of my vision to the screen. Joel Sauter, the lead actor, seamlessly brought his character to life beyond any expectations. Having never written or directed before in this capacity, Apartment 28 was a colossal challenge for me, but it was always grounded in the need to express my subjective experience in embracing identity.

Brennan McGee is a film student at UC Berkeley.

Brennan McGee
B.A. Film & Media Studies, 2018

Faculty Mentor: Mira J. Kopell, Film & Media

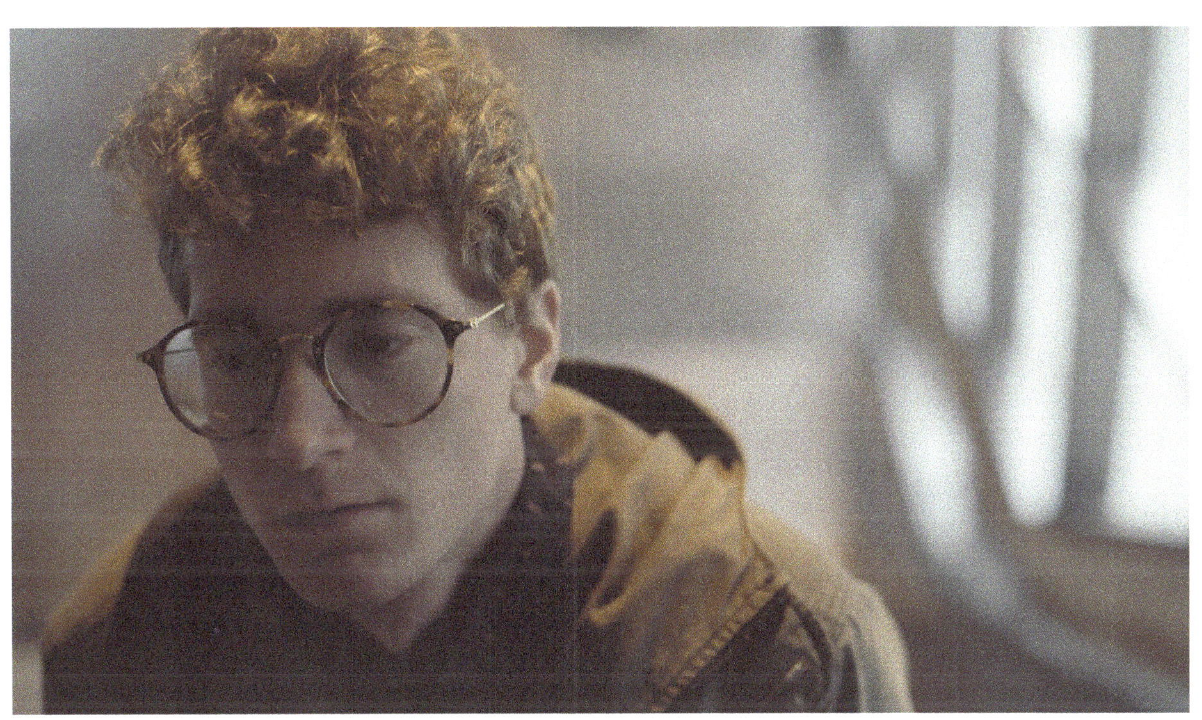

Apartment 28, 2018. Video, 17:24 minutes.

Cade Johnson

Cade Johnson is a third year student majoring in English at UC Berkeley.

Cade Johnson
B.A. English, 2020

Faculty Mentor: Lise Gaston, English

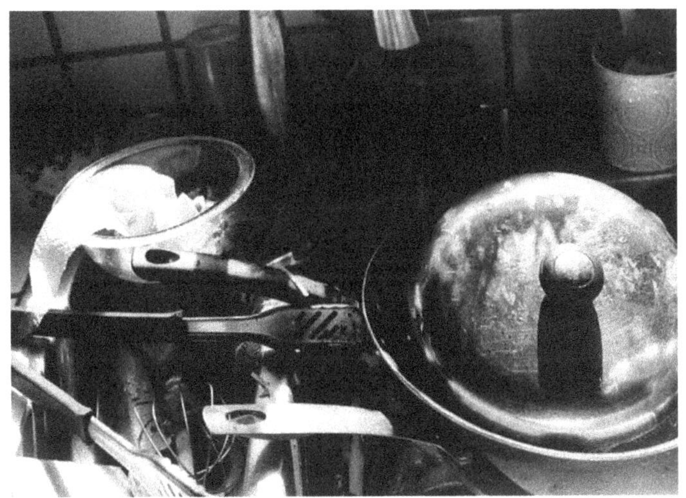

Rise

Morning: the hour of pearl. Time
stops, examines itself, exhales a

sweeping fog, and wakes us. Rooms
glow, light spills and swells like a

flood. Banana and coffee stimulate
the brain's stomach, gingerize

digestion. I sing in the morning,
and I hope you do too. I consider

the constant changing of the
hours, and poetry, and how both

move us in solidarity. We are not
alone in this waking world, so I

flatten my poem with a rolling pin,
slide it in the oven. Watch it rise

"Rise," 2018. Poetry.

Margaret Castro

Margaret Castro is an English major and Creative Writing minor at UC Berkeley.

Margaret Castro
B.A. English, 2018

Faculty Mentor: Lyn Hejinian, English

"Ms. Auften! Ms. Auften! Ma'am, please, stop! Ma'am…" His voice trailed off as the last erratic wave of breath escaped his lungs. He could feel his right knee sock as it rapelled south along the crag of muscle exposed below his knee. The sensation drove him crazy. Had this envelope not been labeled "Next Day" and posted from America, he'd have tossed it at her door, hoped she'd have found it, and yanked the green knit tube back into place. Nothing arrived in Cape Town from the States the next day, and the irony mocked him perilously.

"Hey, hey, relax Bobby. It's ok." She knew he preferred to be called Robert, but the American in her demanded a sense of familiarity, an unspoken display of friendship toward a man with whom she had passed on the street almost every day since her arrival. His nametag had betrayed him. "Who died?"

"Ma'am, please, it's Robert," he pleaded, once again, through spurts of breath. "And how would I know, Ms. Auften? This says your name, not mine."

She reached her hand toward his impatiently unfolded arm, tears of sweat rolling elbow to wrist. A large, flat white envelope clinched between his thumb and middle finger jutted at her with the same anxiety as his manner. Her eyes locked on "Next Day" stamped in patriotic red, a message from the homeland. She looked up at him, smiled at the efforts he'd made, and felt the urge to hug the one person who'd managed to learn her name in the few months she had been in South Africa. It was her intention to be an anonymous transplant, a forgettable face. It moved her.

"Hey, Bobby?" she said as she removed the envelope from his hand.

"Yes, Ms. Auften?"

"You've got to get some new socks."

An hour later, she sat, envelope creeping out of her "I Heart NY" canvas bag. She had only been to New York City once, but here in Cape Town it served as a touchstone to the country from which she came. Lifting her eyes up towards the heavens, she remembered the prickly, humid grass of Central Park making damp spots on her dress, the aroma of wet cement and musty tar after a sudden summer storm. New York was never too far from memory. If there had been more in her savings, she would have moved there. But the truth was she preferred to teach English to get by over working the restaurant circuit in the States. Still, New York felt nothing like Cape Town. Here in her rented single room, an abrupt appendage to a full-sized family home she was bound to by architecture rather than antiquity, she could only marvel at the view. Table Mountain was in the distance. Its rolls of fog reminded her of home on the Pacific Coast of Oregon, and the largish people from whom she was cuddled as a child.

Unlike Bobby, whom she privately regarded as her only acquaintance in town, the anticipation to receive a letter of any sort from home was lost on her. The lone author, she knew, could only have been a brother, Gabriel, three years her senior and troubled beyond the sparse assortment of sunny moments from their childhood. Now as adults, having crossed the threshold of forty, they've surpassed the living age of both their parents, never known relatives outside of one wicked papa on their mother's side, and haven't shared kind words with one another in over a decade. The lightness of the flat, white envelope she held as she pulled the tab open could not possibly know the weight of dread its contents most ardently contained.

"If you are reading these words…" was as far as she got. Auften's hands failed to hold the single, typewritten page any further, her eyes falling as she watched it slink to the floor, a kind of slow-motion accident where the plane's engine ceases but the pilot must wait for impact.

Even she could not understand her body's response. Perhaps it was the astonishment at how a single phrase propelled her into the kind of isolation she sought in Cape Town yet feared in America. Or maybe it was that this letter was no surprise. She knew that one day she would be left behind long before Gabriel ever had the chance to. Or maybe it was the image in her mind of her colossally built, albeit morbidly unstable, brother at a typewriter playing a saturnine game where he occupied the roles of victim and aggressor with delight. In truth, it did not matter much to her.

Days later she finished the entire letter. It was as she imagined: relentless blaming of her not having been there for him (yet she was), anger at her for having left him homeless (yet he wasn't), and the disparate musings of a man who released the reins of life each time he self-terminated his medication. As a result, the only line, other than the first, that affected her was when he signed off, "Love, Gabriel". He wouldn't allow anyone to call him that, except their mom, who would hold him and tell him about the angel he was named after. "God's little messenger", she would say and he would giggle, a brief glimpse of normalcy in his uncharacteristically worked life. He preferred his middle name, John. He used to say that he'd rather be a unique man with a common name than a common man with a unique name. Whatever that meant to him, she knew not.

As she sat by her window, she studied the fog. Its movement was as carefully orchestrated as a ballet, yet cagey in its grandeur. To her, it seemed like waves from the ocean had supplanted themselves in the sky, writhing and winding their way back toward the sea, a mantle of mist tumbling itself dry.

Her phone rang. She reached for it as she would've back home, foolishly instinctive.

"Hello," she said with an imperceptible tremble in her tone.

"Am I speaking with Ms. Auften?" he asked with the same trepidation with which she listened. "Gabriel's sister?"

"Yes, I am both. How may I help?"

"My name is DeAckerly, ma'am, an officer from Florence, Oregon, where your brother lived." The past tense was not lost on her. His hefty voice sounded to her the way she imagined fog would sound: deep and breathy, like an older person in need of some vigor.

"Is he dead?"

Maybe it was her imagination, but there was a quick inhale on the other end of the phone. He intended on calling a relative, not a monster, she thought.

"Yes. He is."

"Has a body been recovered?" Another question that sounded more mandatory than grief stricken. She quietly chastised the blunder.

"One has, yes. Ma'am, are you alone?"

"Yes, why?"

"Well, this news must be very distressing to you, and I'd hate to think there was no one there to comfort you." His voice quivered as it trailed off, like a bow against violin strings. She could hear the genuine care in his voice. It reminded her of her mother.

"I'm fine. A letter arrived from him a few days ago. It implied death." She knew she must have sounded peculiar, both in tone and context.

"Well, ma'am, according to his medical records, you are listed as his only living relative. There is paperwork to be done, assets to transfer." Against her will, she began to laugh. An awkward, guffaw heard mostly in films where a crazy person was being revealed to the hopeful audience.

"Ma'am, are you really ok?"

"I'm sorry. It was the word 'asset,' I hadn't ever thought of him as having any, or being one."

"Should I call back another time?"

"No, no, please, forgive me. Yes, of course I will do whatever you wish."

"We need you to come back, to handle his affairs."

"No."

"You can think about it."

"No. The answer is no."

"But, Ms. Auften…"

"No, I said no. I am not handling his affairs. I have handled his affairs from the time our parents died, over a decade ago. No. I'm sorry." She hung up the phone, as instinctively as she answered it. She looked out of the window and scanned for fog, only to find it had gone back home to the sea. What was left was a great, flat-topped mountain, suspiciously exposed without its hazy cover. They appeared to her precisely how she felt.

Barely a day had passed before the phone rang again. This time she paused before deciding it couldn't be much worse than the last time it had rung. Poor DeAckerly, she thought, just trying to do the right thing, not realizing he was too late for the sympathy he attempted to express.

"Hello?"

"Ms. Auften?" It was the same voice that had received her greeting the last time. "It's DeAckerly, ma'am. I need to ask you again to come home."

She reminded herself to carefully respond, unlike the last time.

"For what, exactly?"

"The paperwork, Ms. Auften. And the removal of assets. You must. We cannot, it's the law."

"Where was the body found? He told me he was homeless before I left."

"He wasn't, he had a home. He rented a condominium on the water. A real nice place. Great views of the ocean." His upbeat spin on the matter unsettled her.

"A home? He had belongings?"

"He did. His place was full of personal effects, photos and the like." Her mind raced. As far as she knew, he was out on the street. She held her response to handle this fresh information.

"There is nothing I need from that place, sir."

"I understand, but what can we do with it? Legally, it all belongs to you."

"Bin it."

"Ma'am, the photos. I assumed you'd at least want those."

"Assumptions only work in science and religion, sir." She sounded insane. He probably assumed she was, just like her brother.

"How did he do it?"

"Do what, ma'am?"

"Kill himself."

"I beg your pardon."

"He was a sick man. I'm aware of that. How did he kill himself?"

"Ms. Auften, I'm sorry if I misled you. Gabriel was on a walk, it would seem, and with the thick fog, the vehicle didn't stop, they must not have seen him. He was found a few hours later, by another driver."

Auften's hand, now cold and pale, reached up toward her mouth, attempting to stifle a cry, or perhaps a gasp. Her eyes shut so tightly the skin crumbled into the tightly bound slits where her eyes were. "But the letter, he sent me a letter."

"I don't know the contents of the letter, but Ms. Auften, your brother did not commit suicide. He was killed."

She opened her eyes and looked again out the window. The sun was beginning to sink towards the horizon, a cool mist being birthed from the sea. Within the hour it would spin like cotton candy and wrap itself around the crown of Table Mountain. A flat crown, but a crown nonetheless. The receiver hung limply in her hand, barely grazing her cheek.

"Sir, I must go."

She hung the receiver up with the gentleness of a potter, aware that her movements could alter the shape of things. This was no time for an episode. Her inclination to rip the phone from the desk and launch it toward her mirror had to be squelched. Her natural instincts to scream and cry and break everything around her, stifled. Her hand dipped into her tote, felt around for the small, cylindrical bottle. The one she hoped would live untouched thanks to her new home, her clean start. With the slightest of pressure, the top came off and she sprinkled not one but two small, round, pale green pills into her palm. A cold gulp of black coffee whooshed them down her throat. A mild, false calm enveloped her.

Twelve hours later, after a bit of rest and time to gather her wits, Auften descended the stairs of her room and out onto the pavement, warmed by the sun. In her tote she carried with her the letter and a passport. A small rectangular suitcase made of faux alligator leather dyed a deep brown hung by her side, thumping sideways against her thigh as she walked. The case itself was nearly empty. Her mother had always advised her to travel light, not realizing the gravity of the counsel she offered considering the baggage she was born to carry. On its return, it would be filled with the last pieces of her natural home. She imagined photos and books, and not much else. It didn't make her sad to envisage this final journey. She welcomed it, in fact, a chance to secure shut a door she never again wished to open. This was more about her than Gabriel. He was an incessant reminder of the sickness inside of her. And now with him gone she could, like the fog, conceal and move through the world with the slow, crawling peace of the mist.

A moment later Bobby appeared from around the corner wearing jeans and a Yankees cap, plainly dressed for his off day. He caught her watching him, his eyes landing on the luggage she held so protectively close to her body. She looked conspicuously guarded, like a child reaching for a flame after being warned against it.

"Ms. Auften, are you going somewhere?" he asked as they stood now facing one another.

"I must go back home. There's been a death."

"Can I help you, ma'am? I will get a cab."

"I will need a cab, Bobby, but first I need to make a stop." Her tone sounded sinister to him, but under the circumstances not too surprising he reconciled.

"I will help you. What do you need?"

"A dress, Bobby. I need a black dress."

She lowered her eyes, but not in sorrow. She slowly raised her stare up towards his face, a quizzical look settled across his brow. "Bobby, will you come with me?"

"Yes, of course, there is a store around the corner." He reached out for her suitcase, the weightlessness in conflict to the moment. "We will find you a dress."

"Bobby?"

"Yes, Ms. Auften?"

"Will you let me buy you some socks?"

He stared at her, at the question. Her head flew back and she let out a laugh so guttural it made his skin quiver. He wondered how she could laugh like that at a time like this. Bobby nodded his head, said nothing, and led her back around the corner.

As they walked, Auften turned her head and looked past Bobby toward the great mountain in the distance. She observed the relentless movement of the fog. The opaque, white vapor formed clouds across the dark, calloused terrain. Back and forth, and back again. Heaven on earth, she thought. She followed Bobby as he gently guided her through a shop doorway. Just past the threshold, her feet froze and she wondered to herself if the fog would wait for her return. She closed her eyes and pictured her brother. The loss of life. The last of her immediate family.

A kind looking woman approached them from the opposite end of the store. Bobby nodded toward a solitary black dress hanging on the rack. Intuitively the woman bowed her head. She had noticed the luggage he was carrying and saw the empty look across Auften's narrow face. Auften walked over to the single black dress and removed it. She held it up and away before placing the hanger below her neck, the way a bride would to imagine herself dressed like a princess on her wedding day.

"I'm going to a funeral," she announced. From somewhere deep inside of her, within the layers of confusion and madness, she stifled the urge to laugh again.

Mail for Bobby, 2017. Fiction, 10 pages.

Nina Djukic

The first lines of this poem came to me when I was, in fact, walking, and really heard the sound of trumpets from my hot and dusty path in the upper ridges of the Berkeley Fire Trails. Its music is in part inspired by T. S. Eliot's famous "Love Song of J. Alfred Prufrock" which has been ringing in my head since I first read it at the age of 14. Like most poems, Love Song is, in part, a poem about poetry, and the act of making: the distance between the poetic speaker and the writer, the struggle to join and find common threads between disparate images, the creation of a world in which sonics are as important as semantics. While seemingly allegorical, the poem was also intended as a backlash against the endless whorl of interpretations that accompany poetics: the dream in fact a dream, the walk in fact a walk, the trumpets in fact trumpets. Though of course ultimately failing to diminish their symbolic potential for readers of the poem, I still wanted to think about the differential significances inherent in and following from such assumptions, even within myself.

Nina Djukic is a recent UC Berkeley graduate who, in college as in life, is torn between a fascination with words and a fascination with bodies. She will be pursuing this second passion in clinical research at UCSF while she works toward a medical degree, hoping to bring her pursuit of poetry with her. She loves to run, read, debate poetic interpretation, swim, sing and grow.

Nina Djukic
B.S. Conservation and Resource Studies, 2018

Faculty Mentor: John Shoptaw, English

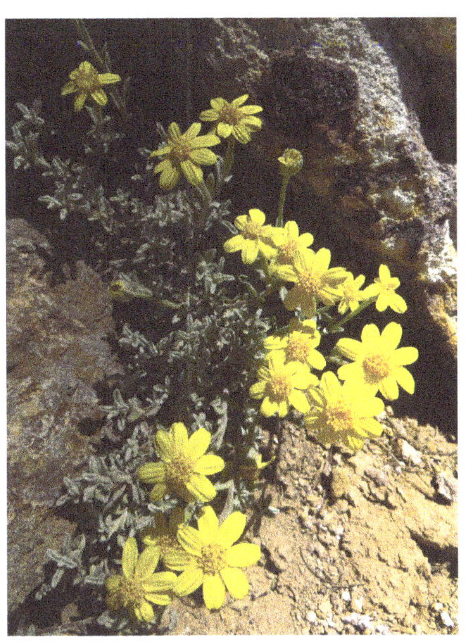

Love Song

        I dreamt that I was
walking. The dusty
        smell of desert
struck me. Then I heard
        the sound of trumpets
from another ridge, the looping,
        pure-note tuning that
once sent beast to battle, that same
        singing sound which toppled
oligarchies now accompanies
        the jazzy musings of
young women in apartment
        buildings re-arranging
flowers in their sweatpants.

        I have driven
to Big Sur; I have watched the light change,
        refract wind and sand off windows,
I have polished doorknobs
        just to see a brighter gold and
watched green apples gleam in the
        heat of a February noon.
I have turned in indecision;
        I have woken to the linger
of a tune.

        Hot and dozing
though I was, I still was walking, still
        could dream: and dreamt
of thick and feather boas draped
        on shoulders in cigar-smoke gloom,
an idle barefoot padding on
        the hardwood or, the whiz of records
whirring, while the sunbeams made
        the carpet bloom
beneath the music
        from another room.

It returned me, and I turned back from
        the wall; slammed the door, said,
it wasn't what I meant, at all;
        said, I treasure my disasters
with my triumphs; my trumpet
        heralds all. Her timbre peals
through windowed streets, lingers
        universally; she sings a symphony
of places, scrawled on candied
        sheets. She sings of blue walls singing
for the sea. I recall a little recklessly
        beneath those pink-and-yellow striped marquees.

            Though I do not think that she
has noticed me. I was
            walking, wandering
the works and days
            of fingers, feet, I was about
to eat, to roll away the years, the stone,
            to clean, to turn, to cross
the bridge—when
            the sound of trumpets
woke me
            from a distant ridge.
Which stands for nothing
            except what it is.

Love Song, 2018. Literature.

Shrey Mendiratta

This untitled work follows the arc of an encounter between two subjects in a series of spaces. In each space, the ritual of encounter flickers, exposing the concurring initial encounter within each of the two subjects' inner landscapes. The film is meant to challenge the embedded understanding of subjectivity between two meeting human beings, bearing themselves to each other, within a prescribed understanding of a separateness between them and the space they occupy. The film moves towards annihilation of these ideas and sensations. Bodies overlap and disappear, leaving four empty landscapes in their wake.

I am me, you are you,
we meet as separate entities,
attempting to find common ground,
ground, we stand atop the ground,
we are not ground,
the ground is beneath us,
we are between it
and what?

Shrey is a recent graduate, interested in film ranging from 16mm experimental pieces to soviet era works. He is currently working on various photography and film projects, steering through a sea of influences, making the works that emerge from a movement in unlearning.

Shrey Mendiratta
B.A. Integrative Biology, 2017

Faculty Mentor: David Borengasser, Film & Media; Colin Brant, Film & Media

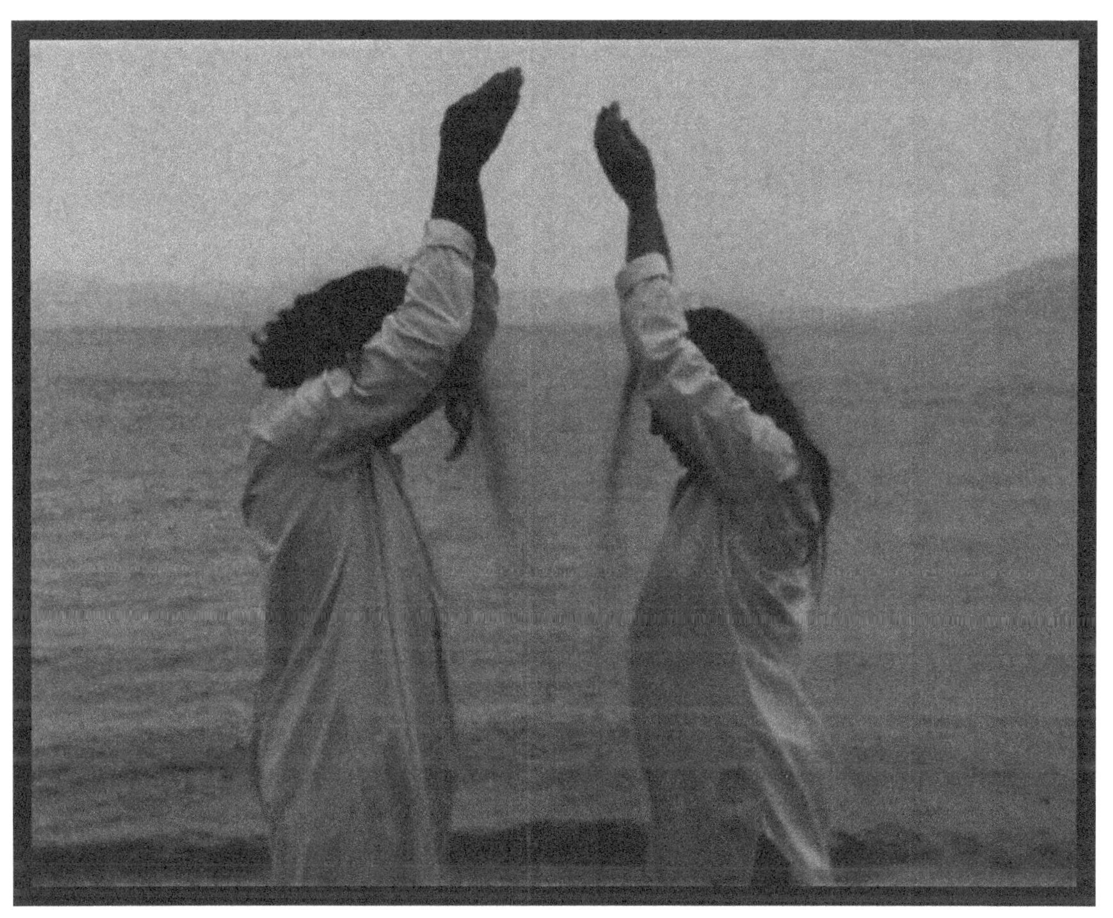

Untitled, 2017. 16mm film, 5:36 minutes.

Yaxuan (Jaden) Chen

In the middle of nowhere, here is Tom. Is he a good guy or a bad guy?

Yaxuan (Jaden) Chen is a Chinese filmmaker who is inspired by Eastern Asian and European cinema.

Yaxuan (Jaden) Chen
B.A. Film, 2019

Faculty Mentor: Jeffrey Skoller, Film & Media

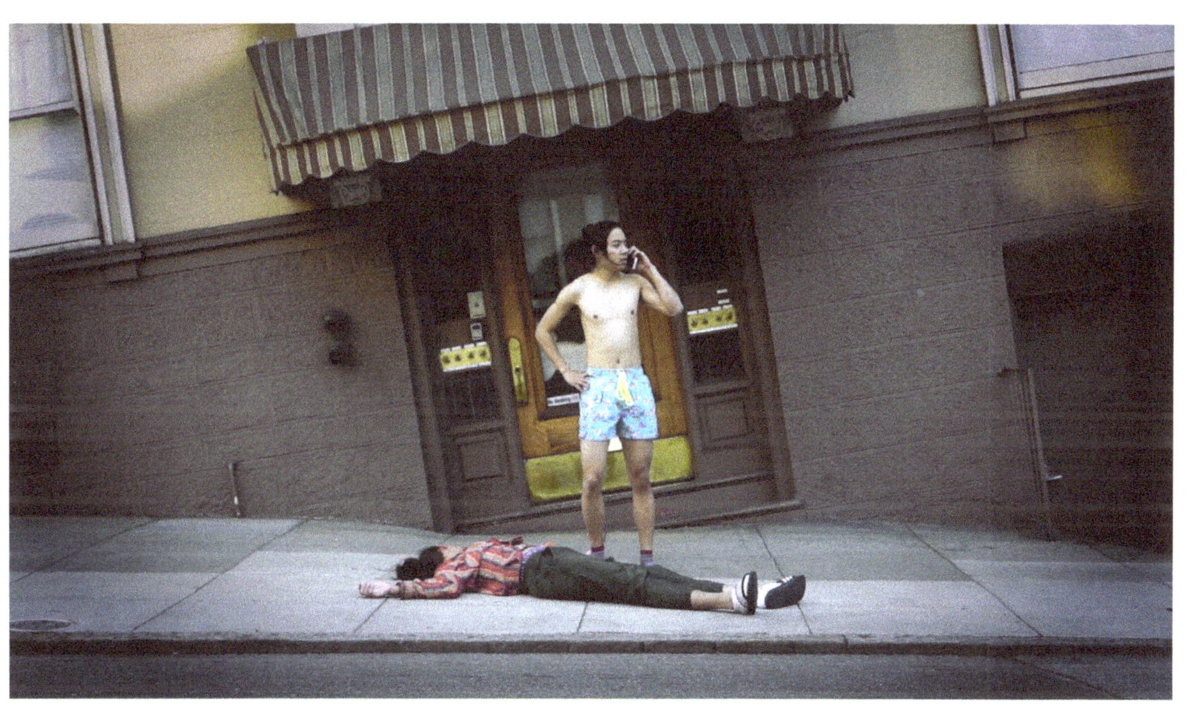

Good to See You, 2017. Video, short film, 5:45 minutes.

CITIES

JOE AYERS
MATTHEW BOWIE
MATTHEW HIDY
PANICAM
SITEWORKS

Joe Ayers

This production of Polaroid Stories by Naomi Iizuka was directed by Margo Hall at UC Berkeley in the spring of 2017. The play blends Ovid's Metamorphoses with the stories of contemporary homeless youth. It was a piece informed by actual interviews with young prostitutes and homeless teens. The text combines poetry and profanity in a way that makes it a great theatrical force. It speaks to the power of storytelling to transform reality. As Margo Hall told us, these are stories of survival. I played d (dionysus) in this production. d is a drug dealer who demands to be worshipped. As Naomi Iizuka explains, d is wild. She told me, "If there is a pulse in this show, d is it."

Joe Ayers is an actor, dancer, choreographer, director, and teaching artist originally from Southern California. His theater credits include productions of Metamorphoses, Polaroid Stories, Reentry: The Process of Resilience, *and* Grease. *His choreography credits include* Heathers: The Musical, Bat Boy: The Musical, The Dream of Kitamura, *and* Cabaret. *He holds three B.A. degrees from UC Berkeley in Theater and Performance Studies; Dance and Performance Studies; and English.*

Joe Ayers
B.A. Theater and Performance Studies;
Dance and Performance Studies; and English, 2018

Faculty Mentor: Margo Hall, Theater, Dance, and Performance Studies

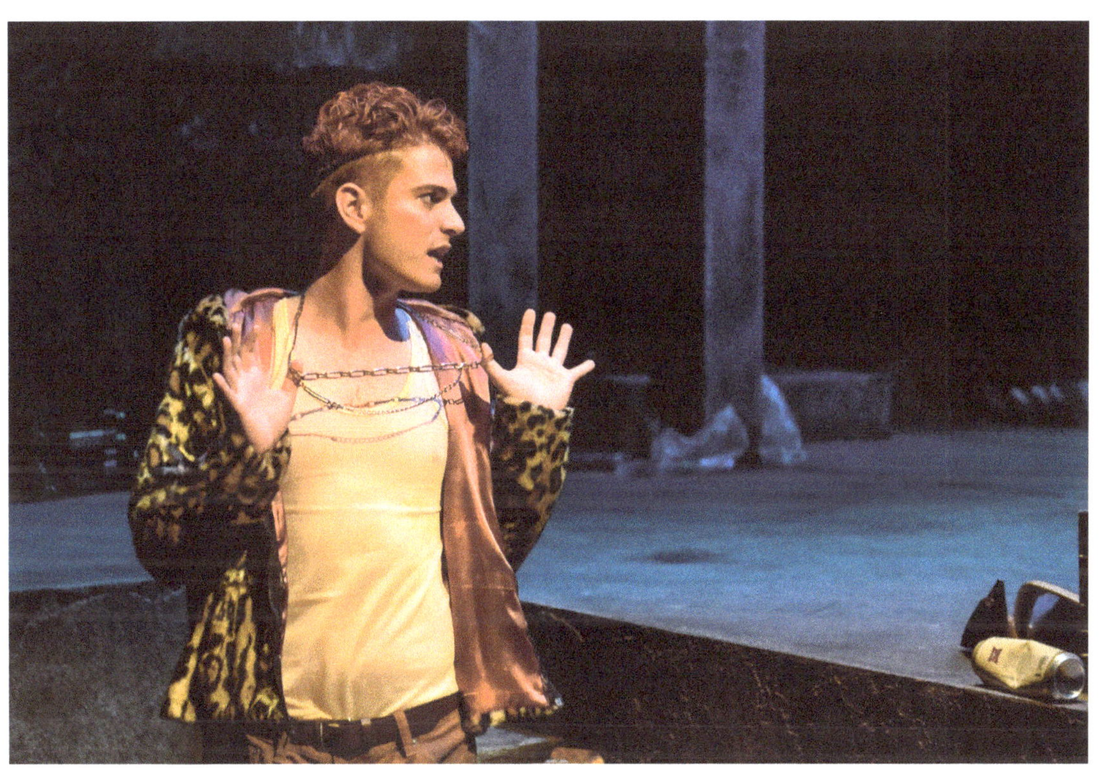

Polaroid Stories, spring 2017. Live performance.

Matthew Bowie

This is a five-part (but fairly brief) lyric—blending text taken from Sharifa Rhodes-Pitts' book Harlem is Nowhere *and Teju Cole's* Open City*—initially meant to represent a conversation between the narrators of those books and overheard by my poem's speaker. The title is a modification of Mahler's song,* Das Lied von der Erde *(The Song of the Earth).*

Recent graduate from the UC Berkeley English Department, former sailor with the United States Navy. California native, aspiring graduate student, and sometime, if failed, pianist.

Matthew Bowie
B.A. English, 2018

Faculty Mentor: Nadia Ellis, African American Studies

Das Leid von der Erde

1.
I greet my neighbors in the street.
I come from a place where you speak to people, and your salutation is a
        sundial,
walking paths cheerfully.
I learned a greeting almost intimate here.
You say: *How you feel?* Or, *How you feeling?* It is not a question from
which you can rush away.

The questions I ask—*Where
is your home? Where are your people from?*—search out origins. The
        answers reveal
a stranger. A stranger stops to ask
if I require direction. I
have lingered too long, or I look uncertain.

2.
Each person must, perhaps being watched, surreal,
by multitudes, assume the room of his own mind
is not, cannot be, a characteristic tic
revealing essential falsehoods, entirely opaque to him. You'll say
nothing, she said. Things don't go away just because you choose
to forget it only needs

to happen once. The just risen sun came at
the Hudson at such an acute angle that the river
gleamed. Of course, it burned him. He carried the resulting scar.

The initial awareness of pain was gone, there was no mortal.
They left, sprinting; they left and time's shape was restored. People, the
last fragments of the afternoon's tasks, people, but there
were none, just the dry wind falling through the trees.

The intricacy of the weeds startled. Each appeared
to be intent on his own thought, our being "brothers."

3.
They passed, and the lack
of nods felt choreographed
and white—a glance from each askance and two half-assed side steps,

except, as he went past and gazed up, she paused yawned and looked
back

wrote down in her book the cut of his shirt. He hummed a three note
motive

and thought on his hurt.

4.
There were self-published books, dashikis, posters on black
liberation, djembe drums, drivers of the black livery
cabs, early-twentieth-century lynchings of African
American photographs, awaiting the fares they could pick
up off the clock. These survivors would also come to be
forgotten. Young men in hooded sweatshirts, the denizens of an informal
economy, passed messages to each other, enacting

a choreography opaque to all but themselves.
It was careless thinking to draw the link too easily
and the sky and the river were a single darkly misted sheet
and the horizon had vanished. In the Harlem night, there were no whites.
Surrender—negotiation—played a role in this.

5

To the memory of... you cannot read
in whose memory this work was made. You must be looking down to see
        them, or be otherwise disconnected. I crossed
an alternate path, walking that way,
just, in order to see the street.
It was late summer when I first saw:
elaborate messages, sidewalk writings
in the pavement, on brightly colored chalk.
Love yourself. Your life is worth saving.
Reality will outlast
you. And though they were designed to be destroyed, I felt compelled to
        preserve.

Das Leid von der Erde, 2016. Poetry.

Matthew Hidy

Light Isle *is a collection of some of the remaining Bay Area Neon Signs that dot the landscapes I frequent. In a time where LCD and fluorescent lights have replaced a method for making lighted signs, the rare surviving neon signs stand apart from modern lighted signs in their material characteristics and the history they connote. I suggest the notion of neon as a medium by emphasizing its simplicity, vibrancy, and famous luminescence.* Light Isle *questions that if neon's distinct characteristics allow its recognition as a distinct medium, then do other formats of visual and audio mediums prominently suggest their unique differences? I argue that the respective defining characteristics of celluloid film and digital video are critical formal elements of each and not equivalent. Formats of media have followed a trend of synthesis and convergence instead of emphasizing individual strengths. Neon in* Light Isle *serves to defend its presence in the Bay Area and globally, as a unique treasure of our streets.*

Matthew is an undergraduate senior at UC Berkeley majoring in Film Studies and a prospective film archivist. He has been interested in film since he got a 8mm movie camera when he was fifteen years old and continues to work in 8mm and 16mm. He has a love for archival film presentations and shows 16mm and 35mm film at home in conjunction with his film club. Other interests of his include record collecting and historic preservation, both of which directly influenced his film Light Isle.

Matthew Hidy
B.A. Film, 2019

Faculty Mentor: David Borengasser, Film & Media; Colin Brant, Film & Media

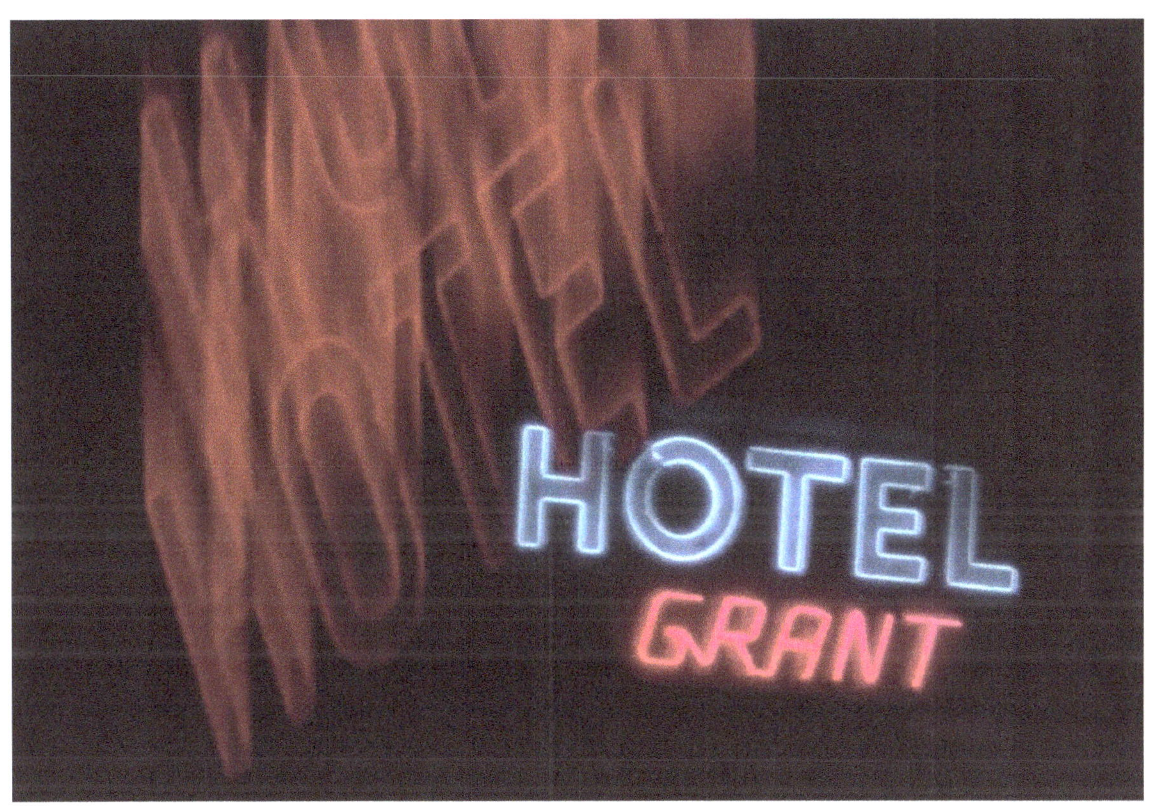

Light Isle, 2017. 16mm film, 4:02 minutes.

PaniCam

Designed for the realities of life in an urban setting, PaniCam is a wearable device hidden on the back of one's collar which helps the wearer safely journey home at night. Using a modular design that can be fitted to any jacket-like item of clothing, PaniCam contains a camera, a Piezo speaker and an alarm light system, helping the wearer feel secure by providing video footage of a potential assailant, while emitting light and sound in order to scare the assailant away. PaniCam is contained within the collar of the wearer's jacket, and is activated as soon as the wearer feels like she or he is in a potentially dangerous situation. By popping their collar, the wearer activates the camera, recording the potential assailant and environment behind the wearer. Should the assailant make a move, the wearer can then activate an audible and visual alarm via a small capacitive touch button located on the front tip of the collar. Discrete and subtle, PaniCam is a solution to the dangerous realities of walking alone at night.

The group comprised three graduate graduate students and one undergraduate senior, bringing in a variety of skills in design thinking, Human Centered Design, 3D modeling, laser cutting, 3D printing and electronics.

Kiran Delneuville
M.A. Global Studies, 2018

Nisha Pathak
MIMS UI/UX and Product Design, 2018

Purva Juvekar
M.Eng. Mechanical Engineering, 2018

Yayu Zheng
B.A. Film and Media Studies, 2018

Faculty Mentor: Eric Paulos, Electrical Engineering Computer Science

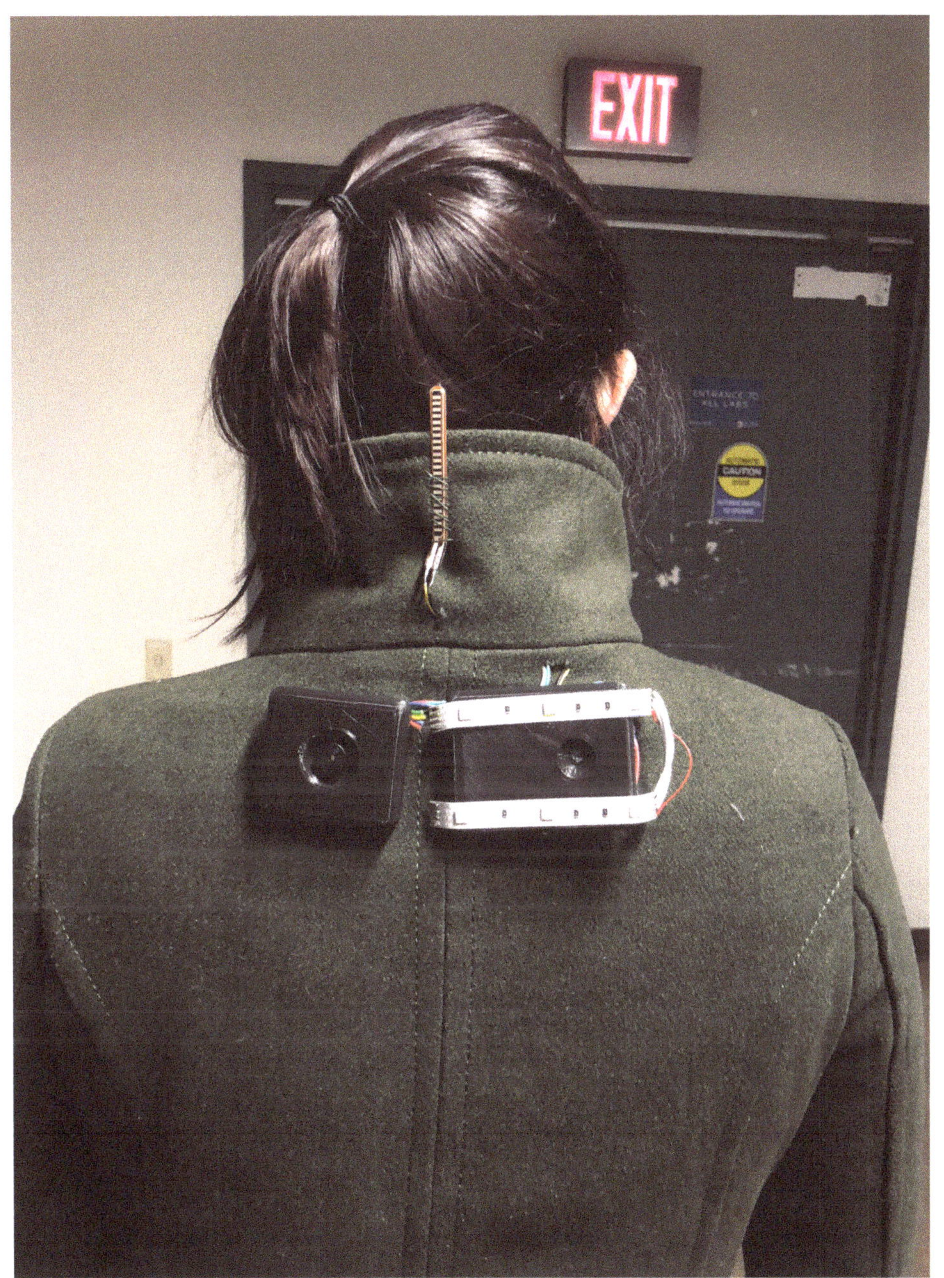

PaniCam, spring 2018. Hardware.

Siteworks

We "Siteworkers" created a site-specific performance in order to research and share a contested public space known as the Albany Bulb. The Bulb is a construction debris landfill in San Francisco Bay known for its informal art, spectacular views, and for many years, a longstanding homeless community. We drew maps of its physical and emotional landscape and created a performance to allow a small invited audience to share in our explorations. Our goal was to examine the notion of public space as a commons. Our research combined methods from landscape architecture, urban design, city planning, archaeology, literary analysis, dance, and theater. The performance that grew out of the research was immersive, playful, participatory, and highly personal. We invited our guests/audience to a "surprise party" and walked them through the nooks and crannies of the Bulb as they picked wildflowers, made garlands and pondered park regulations. They played with mirrors, shared food, listened to music, and watched a lone dancer on a distant dike, silhouetted against a view of the Golden Gate. We shared our understanding of the Bulb as a place where park users have created a commons with complicated thresholds between the public and the private.

The production team was highly interdisciplinary, including students majoring in Anthropology, Architecture, Art Practice, Art History, Conservation and Resource Studies, Development Studies, Film and Media Studies, Political Science, Theater, Dance & Performance Studies, and Urban Studies. Each student brought perspectives and habits of thought from their home discipline and we learned a lot from each other's approaches. We were also asked to bring a personal "superpower" as a resource to benefit the group. These superpowers included cooking, listening, patience with minute crafting projects, playing the Chinese zither, and being able to run really fast. The research and performance was done as part of the course Siteworks: Understanding Place Through Design and Performance (Landscape Architecture 154/Theater 154) and was sponsored by the Global Urban Humanities Initiative. The process is chronicled at https://albanybulbsiteworks.wordpress.com/

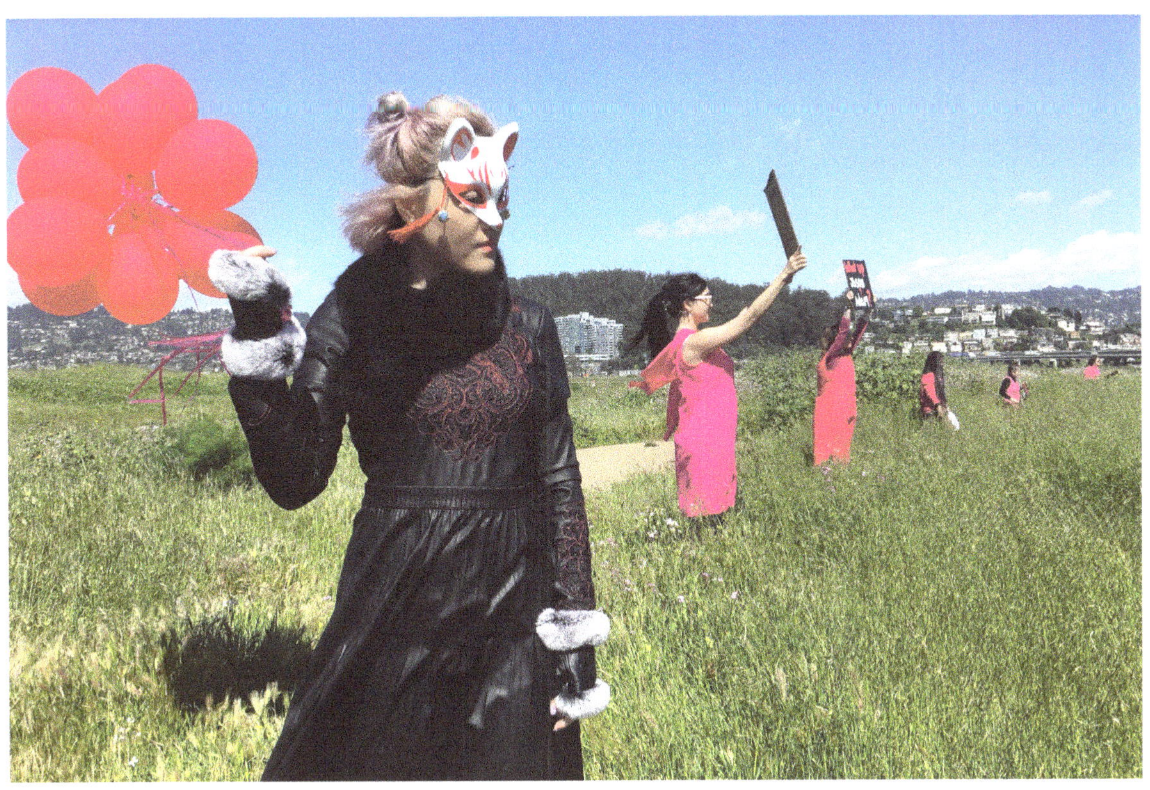

Siteworks: You're Invited, 2018. Live performance, 2 hours.

Aniston-Maylee Breslin
B.A. Art History, 2018

Helen Jiang
B.A. Film and Media
Studies, 2018

Amy Loo
B.A. Political Science,
2018

Tiffany Meng
B.A. Urban Studies, 2019

Ricky Montali
B.A. Art Practice, 2018

Kathleen O'Connor
B.A. Theater, Dance, and
Performance Studies, 2018

Patricia Midy
B.A. Individual Major,
Space and Character, 2019

Moira Peckham
B.A. Anthropology and
Archaeology, 2018

Michael Qi
B.A. Undeclared, 2021

Peihan Qian
B.A. Architecture, 2020

Hannah Ricker
B.A. Development Studies,
2018

Natalia Rico
B.S. Conservation and
Resource Studies, 2019

Briana Salmon
B.A. Architecture, 2018

Daniel Sanchez
B.A. Architecture, 2018

Grace Treffinger
B.S. Conservation and
Resource Studies, 2018

Faculty Mentors: Ghigo DiTommaso, Landscape Architecture and
Environmental Planning; Erica Chong Shuch, Theater, Dance, and Performance
Studies; Susan Moffat, City and Regional Planning, Global Urban Humanities
Initiative. Graduate Student Mentor: Annie Danis, Archaeology/Anthropology

ENVIRONMENT

ALVARO AZCÁRRAGA
FANTASTICK
FLIPPER FILTER

Alvaro Azcárraga

SEMO is a company that was made as both a visual thought-experiment in order to break down the complexity of our current foodscape and a critique on how we preserve culture in today's dynamic environment.

The SEMO Soil Laboratory focuses on: (1) The collection and analysis of soil samples in our SEMO SOIL CORE CONTAINERS; (2) The visualization, genetic testing and analysis of any micro-organisms (bacteria, fungi, protozoa, nematodes) as well as any potential macro-organisms (arthropods and earthworms); and, (3) Returning information to communities as well as incorporating it into the SEMO database.

Alvaro's work takes an interdisciplinary path, incorporating elements of sculpture, ceramics, performance, and installation. His work addresses themes related to a cultural identity and what it means for it to become global, the progress of technology, food systems, manufacturing, and scientific research, among others. He grew up in Mexico City and was enveloped in a globalized environment.

Alvaro Azcárraga
B.A. Art Practice and Molecular & Cell Biology, 2018

Faculty Mentor: Brody Reiman, Art Practice; Stephanie Syjuco, Art Practice

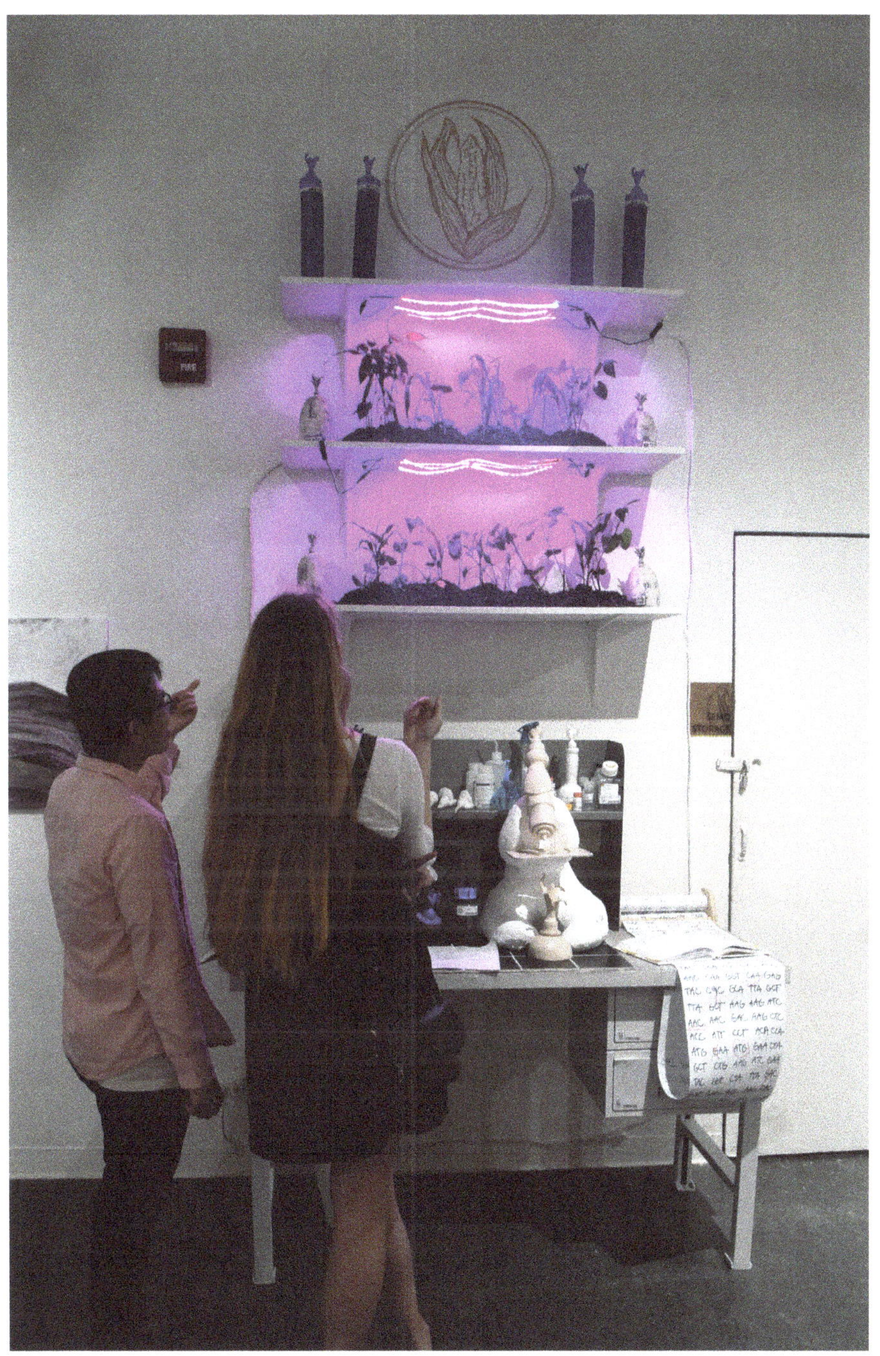

SEMO Soil Laboratory, 2018. Ceramics, soil, found table, laser-cut wood, plaster and ceramics microscope, books, laser engraved ceramic tile, zea mays, phaseolus vulgaris, cucurbita pepo var. Cylindrica, LED Plant Lights, shelves, found bookcase, miscellaneous scientific equipment. Variable dimensions.

FantaSTICK

The phrase "children are naturally scientists" is one we hear often. And yet, these innate qualities in children may be hindered by a new and obsessive attachment to mobile devices and applications. This shift has had detrimental effects on children, including obesity, decreased attention spans and poor academic performance. As a response, we developed FantaSTICK, a fun tool that augments the classroom experience for children, through guidance and structure that can support their natural curiosity and activity and ultimately empower them to engage with the outdoors (like scientists) rather than their mobile devices. FantaSTICK is divided into detachable modules corresponding to colors and tasks.

The FantaSTICK team is a group of graduate and undergraduate students at UC Berkeley, comprising of an interdisciplinary team made up of engineers, designers, and artists. They came together during their Critical Making class to bridge digital and physical worlds and envision new ways for children to interact and experience nature.

Arnaud Bard de Coutance
M.Eng, 2018

Silvia Kim
B.A. Cognitive Science, 2018

Lieyah Dagan
B.A. Interdisciplinary Studies, 2018

Alyssa Li
MIMS, 2019

Faculty Mentor: Eric Paulos, Electrical Engineering Computer Science

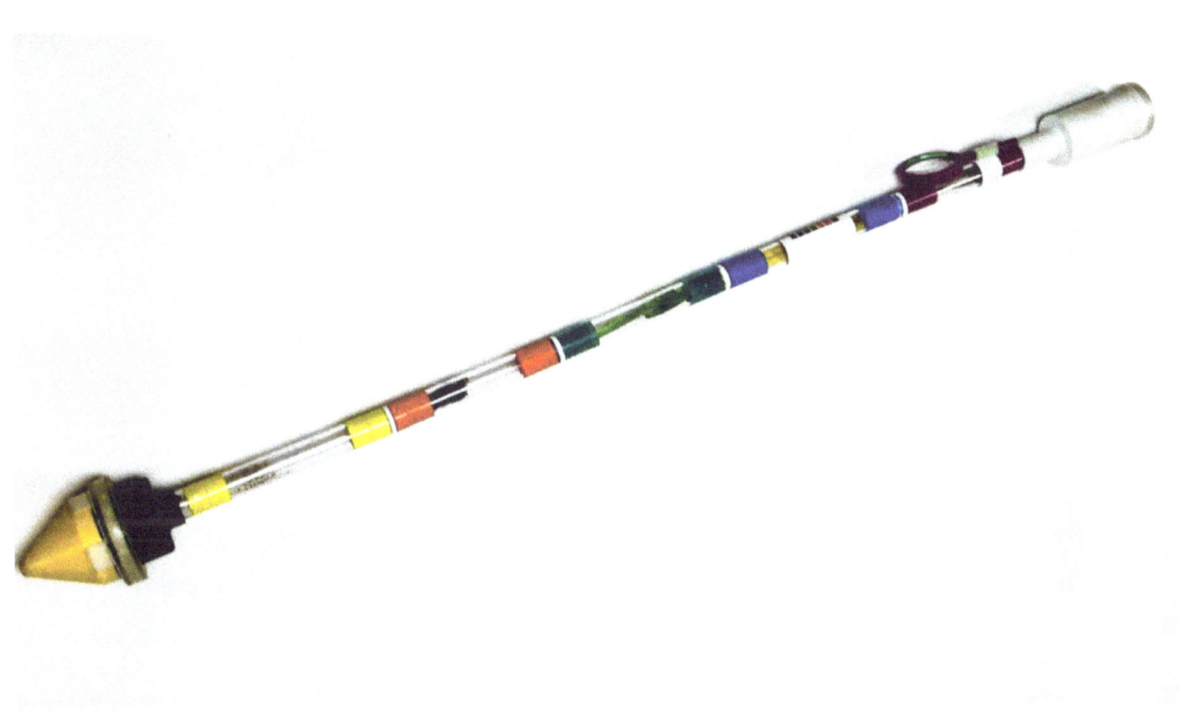

Fantastick, 2018. Polycarbonate tubing, 3D printed PLA, 2 x 2 x 5 in.

Flipper Filter

Flipper Filter *is an economically and environmentally friendly device designed to help clean the oceans of microplastics and protect marine fauna. Flipper Filter's structural ridges are dictated by the morphological tectonics of leatherback sea turtles. Its bioinspired design allows for more efficient maneuverability in the water. Flipper Filter also takes inspiration from filter feeding baleen whales. Just as baleen whales take in ocean water and use their tongue to capture food, Flipper Filter will receive ocean water containing microplastics and trap the polluting microplastics.*

The Flipper Filter team are two undergraduates from architecture and biology with a shared passion for the new dimensions of design possible with biomimetics. In combining their different skills and knowledge, they developed this project with the aim of creating an economically efficient device that could be a commercial product as well as a device to benefit society. They started by examining marine animals and their movement mechanisms and found the most energy and cost efficient geometric morphology for swimming in the ocean in the leatherback sea turtle. Due to their different backgrounds and collaboration of ideas, they were able to produce an invention to help reduce microplastic pollution and potentially diminish a marine and human health hazard.

Tia LaMore
B.S. Integrative Biology, 2020

Reem Makkawi
B.A. Architecture, 2018

Faculty Mentor: Robert J. Full, Integrative Biology

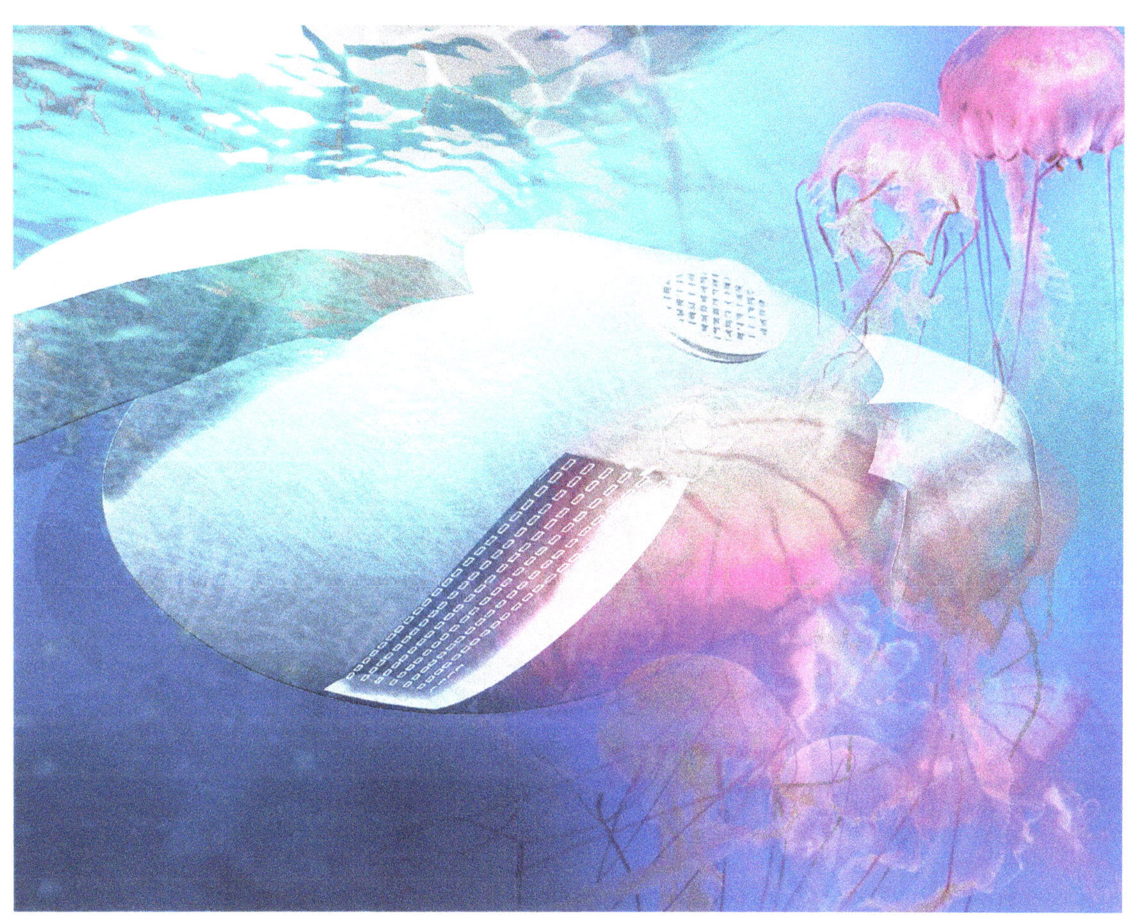

Flipper Filter: A Bioinspired Robot Preserving Marine Life, 2018. Wood, fabric and chipboard for the model, modeled in Rhino and laser cut. For the images: Rhino, Photoshop and Illustrator, 1:1 scale wood model.

FABRICATION

Alexandra Grabow

All in the Timing is a compilation of playwright David Ives' four wittiest one-act works. The fantastic four chosen included Sure Thing, Time Flies, English Made Simple *and* Universal Language. Sure Thing *explores the possibilities of conversation as couple Bill and Betty try (and fail) to connect with each other; however, when one of the punchy pair gives an undesirable response, their conversation is reset with the ringing of a bell. In* Time Flies, *the audience flutters into the lives of two mayflies, May and Horace, on a first date as they discover they do not have as much time to chat and drink "swamp water" as they once thought. In* English Made Simple, *The Narrator, who is a sharp as a tack, guides party-goers Jack and Jill through the intricacies of grammar. Finally, learn "Unamunda" in* Universal Language, *as Don attempts to swindle a shy young woman afflicted with a speech impediment, promising her a life without pause.*

Alexandra is a third-year Art Practice, and Theater and Performance Studies major. Originally an intended Architecture major, Alexandra was liberated by the knowledge that "nothing must be permanent" in theater and found that her passion for Art Practice complemented her scenic artistry. With a new interest in portraiture, Alexandra found herself exploring how the interpretation of facial expressions are understood in a variety of environments. While working on All in the Timing, *her fascination with pointillism conjured the idea of incorporating small LEDs into the brick wall facing.*

Alexandra Grabow
B.A. Art Practice and Theater and Performance Studies, 2020

Faculty Mentor: Annie Smart, Theater, Dance, and Performance Studies

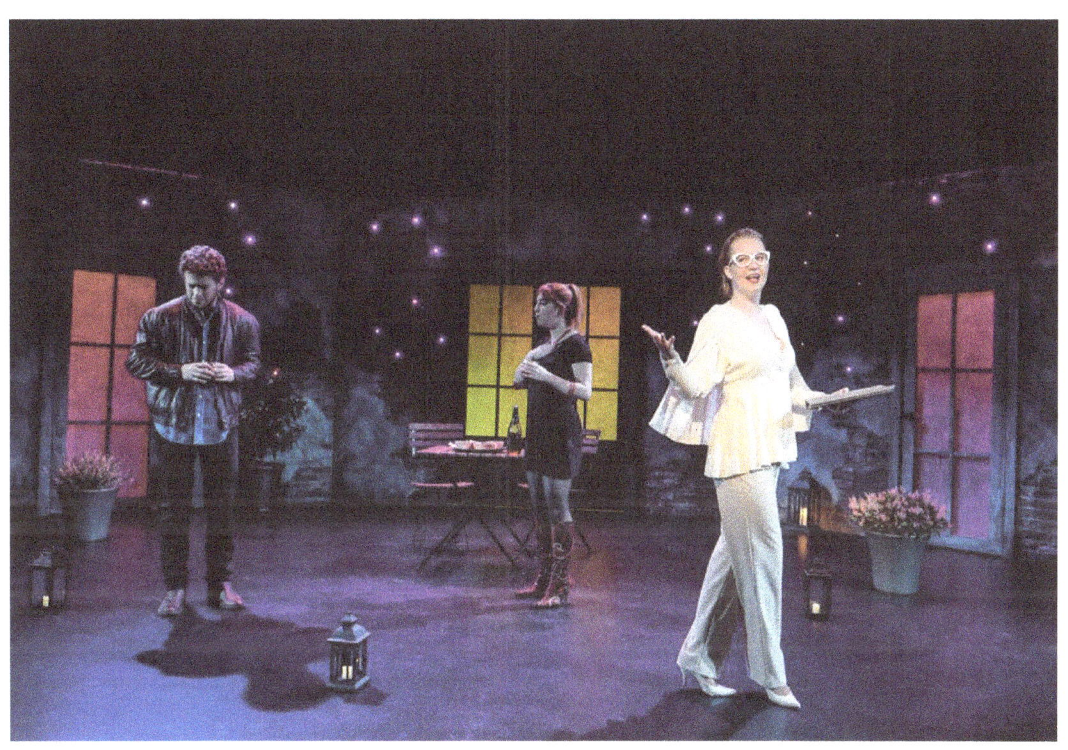

All in the Timing: An Evening of Short Comedies by David Ives, March 15-18, 2018.
Live performance, 1 hour 15 minutes.

Cantilevered Stairs

When presented with the challenge of designing and constructing a steel cantilevered platform, our group decided to use the structural integrity of a truss to highlight the strength and lightness of steel. Beginning with a typical seven-inch riser and eleven-inch tread, the resultant angle was then manipulated in various ways to produce an abstracted truss system that supports the stair and makes it appear to be floating in space. The design process took place over a two-week period, while the time spent in the fabrication shop on construction was four days. We first cut down our square tube steel and sheet metal into the appropriate sizes, before welding the frame together, and finally attaching the sheet metal treads by use of rivets.

The team met through Arch 160, Introduction to Construction, a required class for all architecture majors. Prior to this course, as a group, they had very little experience working in construction so they were excited to embrace this opportunity and participate in a design build project.

Chutikarn Cholsaipan
B.A. Architecture, 2019

Jacqueline Serrano
B.A. Architecture, 2019

Viet Nguyen
B.A. Architecture, 2019

Camille Vistica
B.A. Architecture, 2019

Faculty Mentor: Jamay Li, Architecture

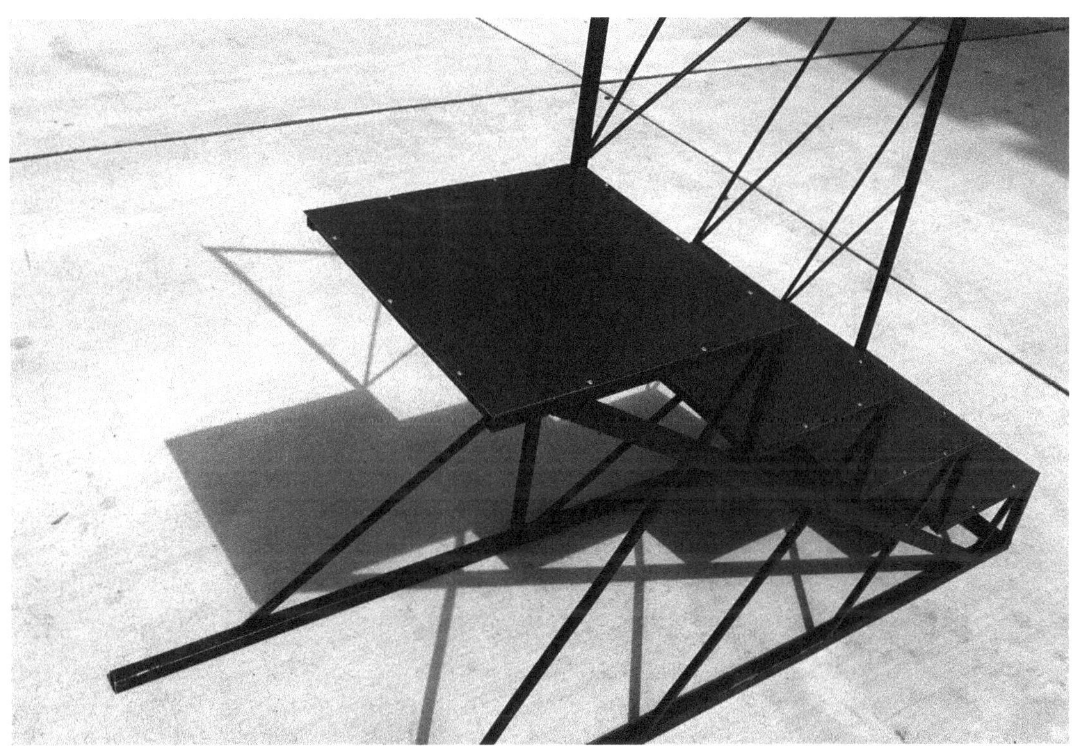

Cantilevered Stairs, 2018. HSS steel and sheet metal, 60 x 24 x 60 in.

Concrete Puzzle

Inspired by puzzle games, the two concrete pieces slot into one another through the square 6" opening and key. As a result, the two pieces can be rotated and rearranged to the user's preferences to become a mini table with various height changes.

The Concrete Puzzle team are two senior Architecture students at UC Berkeley. They both believe in simple but complex design and used this as a strategy in the design for this project.

Setareh Barimani
B.A. Architecture, 2018

Natya Admira Dharmosetio
B.A. Architecture, 2018

Faculty Mentor: Jordan Cayanan, Architecture

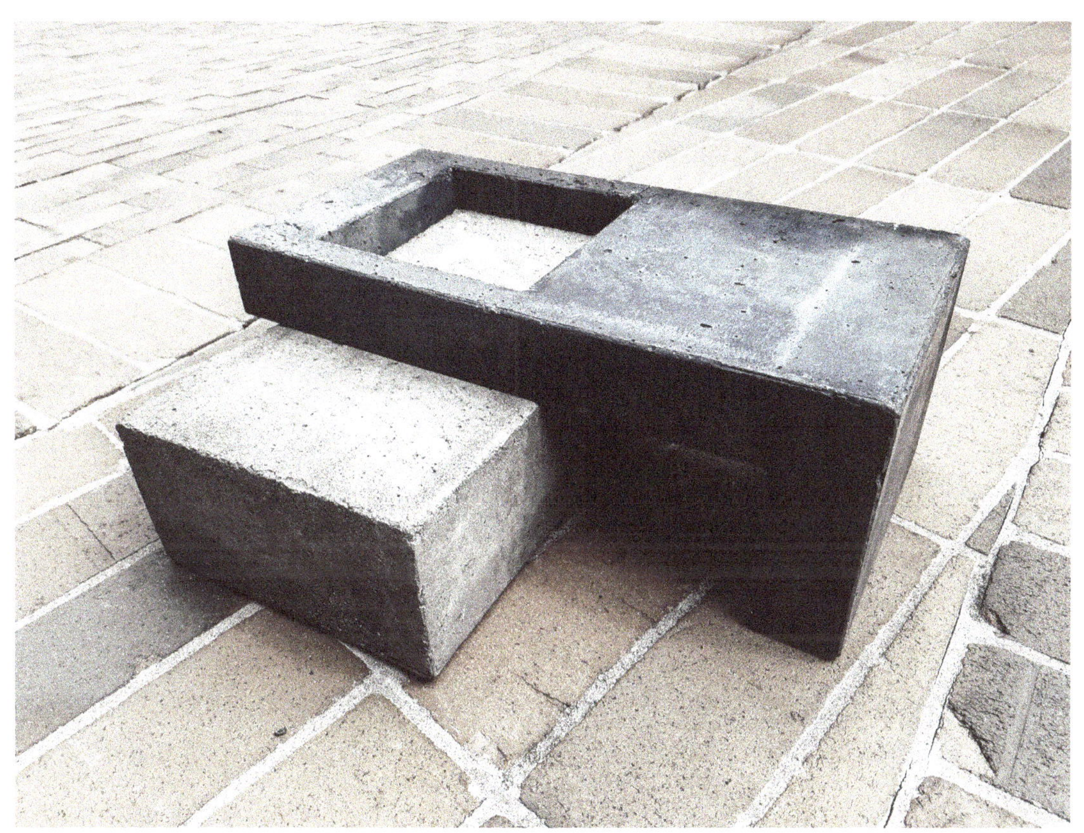

Concrete Puzzle, 2018. Concrete, 16 x 8 in.

Kickstarter

Kickstarter is a dynamic, assistive kickboard equipped with interactive technology to assist with swimming education, helping beginning swimmers learn to navigate obstacles and swim with the proper straight-legged kicking technique. The ultrasonic sensor embedded into the front of the kickboard detects walls, people, and other obstacles; a motor provides haptic feedback via a vibration motor under the hand-holds in order to allow the swimmer to maneuver and avoid collisions. The flex sensor in the knee-pad detects bending in the knees during freestyle kicks and uses radio communication with LED lights in the kickboard to provide feedback on kicking technique. The lights turn green when the user is exhibiting proper kicking technique, yellow with minimal bending, and red if knees are too bent. The Kickstarter kickboard is perfect for amateurs that are learning to master great kicking technique, using real-time interactive technology to provide feedback and augment the swimming education experience.

This project was created as part of the Jacobs Institute course, Critical Making. Team Kickstarter worked in groups to ideate and develop a prototype for the challenge of collaging a simple human power transportation technology with a novel interactive experience. The primary constraints were that the transportation device must be human powered and embed, attach, or augment sensing and relevant electronic output modalities to the transportation device. The final design also had to use some form of wireless technology to connect with outside data sources. The interdisciplinary team of undergraduate students had four weeks to develop this project, including user research, ideation, and prototyping.

Arianna Ninh
B.A. Cognitive Science, 2019

Varna Vasudevan
B.S. Mechanical Engineering, 2019

Essie Xu
B.A. Economics, 2019

Faculty Mentor: Eric Paulos, Electrical Engineering Computer Science

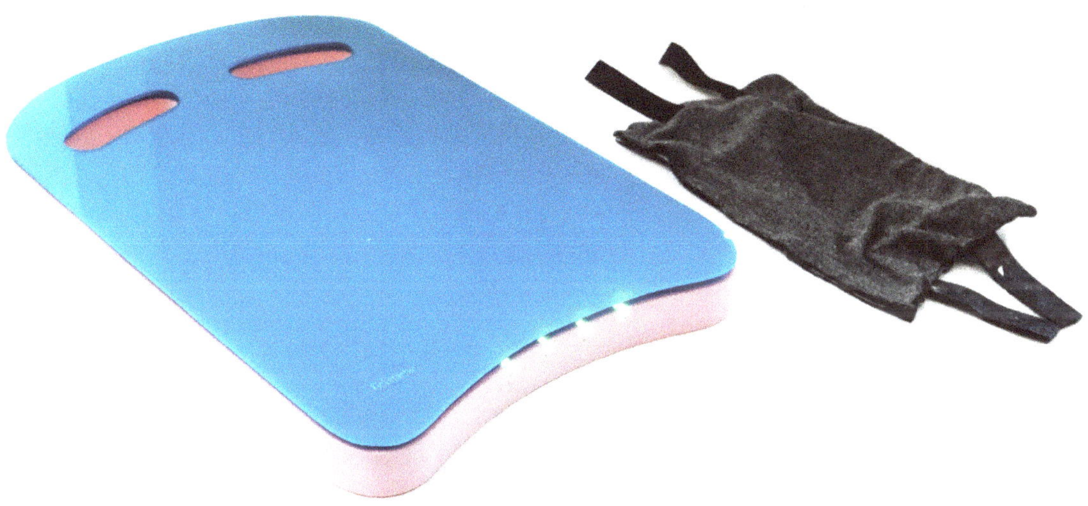

Kickstarter, 2018. Laser-cut wood, styrofoam, Arduino, Kickboard: 2 x 1.5 ft; Knee Pad: 5 x 10 in.

Le Stair

Tasked with building a cantilevered platform at the end of a set of stairs, our team sought to push the envelope. The use of a single uniform material permitted for a near transparency of the volume and an ability to explore the articulation of structural and design elements more thoroughly. Using such a thin metal rod for building material forced us to be very meticulous with structural decisions. We also had to make very rigid and exact welds so that crucial connections would not fail. Looking at the final design, the fluctuating and repetitive form of the hand rail creates an illusion of imbalance, in juxtaposition with the concise structural support below the treads. The stark orange color allows the structure to stand out against its surroundings.

This group consists of Brenda Delgado-Barajas, Elizabeth Romo, Jonathan Solis, and David Musa. All four are undergraduates in their final semester of the CED's Architecture program. Brenda, Elizabeth, and Jonathan are graduates of Cosumnes River College, who transferred to UC Berkeley for their junior and senior years. David has attended Cal for four years.

Brenda Delgado-Barajas
B.A. Architecture, 2018

Elizabeth Romo
B.A. Architecture, 2018

David Musa
B.A. Architecture, 2018

Jonathan Solis
B.A. Architecture, 2018

Faculty Mentor: Dana Buntrock, Architecture; David Jaehning, Architecture; Jeremy Ferguson, Architecture

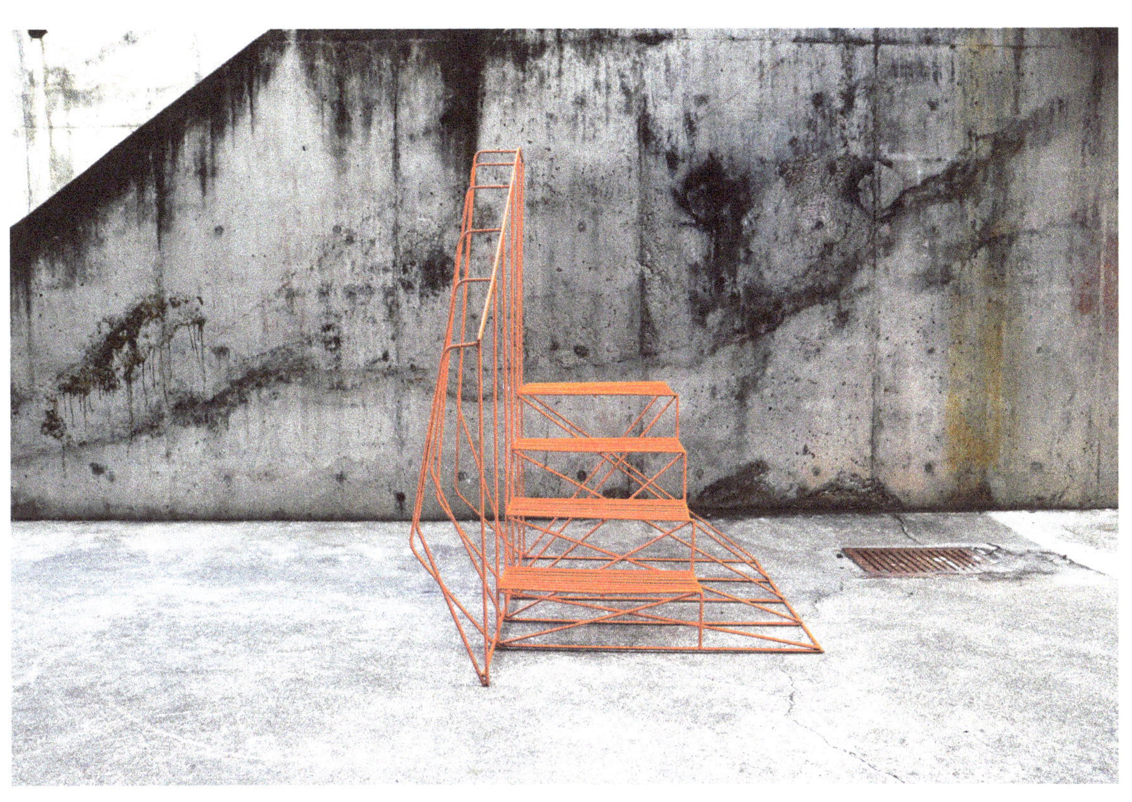

Le Stair, 2018. Paint on welded steel, 8 x 5 x 5.5 ft.

Morphosis

This project required us to work with others to design and construct a planter box. The objective was to introduce us to wood and how joints work together. We were graded based on our design and how well we constructed our planter box according to materials, simplicity, and craft. Our design resulted from various study models. Our final design was organic in the way that we decided to design this model along the way instead of being confined to a digital model. We built a grid of ½" x ½" long members and decided to have the box morph into something else as if the design was breaking out of the box. Using Douglas fir, we created a grid that mimics pixelation and morphs into pieces of varying lengths. Dowels and glue were used as our joint connections.

Team Morphosis is made up of of Benzi Blatman, Natasha Landicho, Cody Lambrecht and Lana Dementsova. They collectively agreed on Benzi's idea for the final design of the planter box to be morphing out of a conventional 3D grid. Natasha provided the wood from scrap yards and other materials to ensure they spent no money on this project. With a background in wood-working, Cody's skills helped construct the planter box as efficiently as possible. Lana provided wine corks for the legs of the planter box so it would not scrape the ground.

Benzi Blatman
B.A. Landscape Architecture, 2020

Cody Lambrecht
B.A. Architecture, 2019

Lana Dementsova
B.A. Architecture, 2019

Natasha Landicho
B.A. Urban Studies, 2020

Faculty Mentor: Dana Buntrock, Architecture

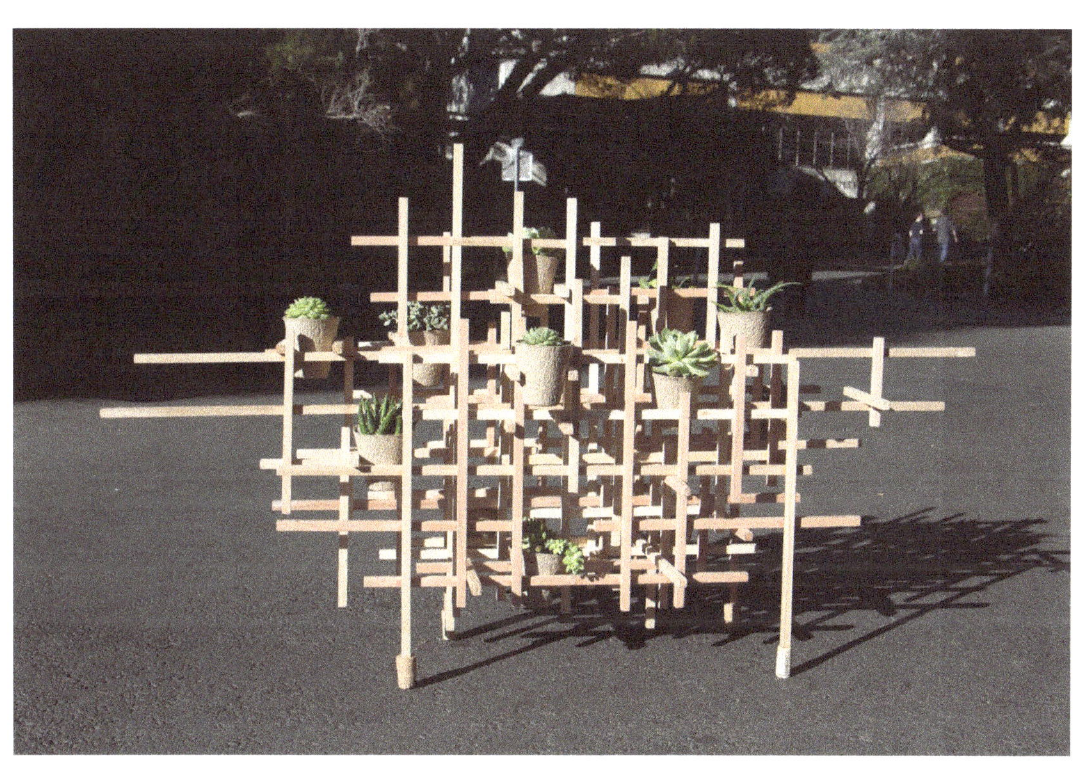

Morphosis: Planter Box, 2018. Wood, 48 x 24 x 8 in.

Polygonal Fireplace

The project explores concrete as a fire-resistant and versatile material. Concrete has no inherent form of its own, therefore, allows for forming a void easily. Our design adopts two approaches to create holes on concrete slab. The hole in the middle serves as a place for bonfire, and the other on the concrete slab performs as a grill to place the food. We use wood panels to create its formwork. Vertical wood panels are fastened to a heavy base by screws, and concrete is poured in gaps between two sides of panels. The ratio of water and cement is carefully designed to create a brutal texture for the fireplace.

Team Polygonal Fireplace *is an international group composed of three students. Delphina Wedell and Josselenn Maldonado are second-year architecture student at Berkeley. Rui Wang is a third-year architecture concurrent-enrollment student from Harbin Institute of Technology, China.*

Josselenn Maldonado
B.A. Architecture, 2020

Rui Wang
CED-GAP, 2020

Delphina Wedell
B.A. Architecture, 2020

Faculty Mentor: Dana Buntrock, Architecture; Nikita Tugarin, Architecture

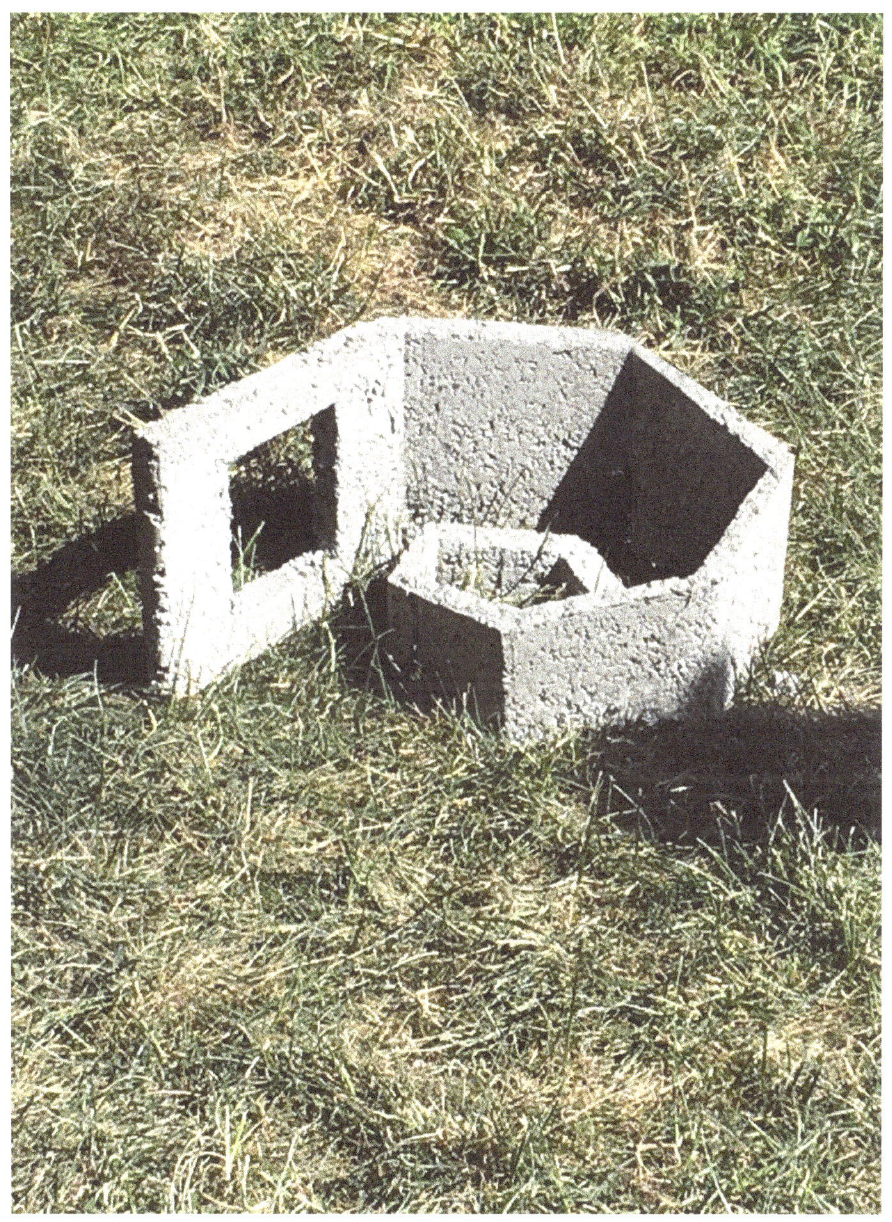

Polygonal Fireplace, 2018. Wood panels, 18 x 18 x 11 in.

The Wood Planter Project

The design includes two main components, the box and the plank. Understanding that plants grow, perhaps someday needing bigger pots, our design is motivated to accommodate the growth of plants. The planter is designed so that it does not have any designated or prescribed place or size for pots to sit into, and that the plank is movable side-to-side through the slats of the box, which is adjustable to the necessary space for pots and the liking of the user. The slatted, simplistic and minimalistic design scheme aims for maximum spacing, exposure to sunlight, but especially for versatility, such that it could function as other items in a house, like a mini shelf or stool.

Team Wood Planter is made up of three Architecture students from UC Berkeley. They believe in simple but complex design and use this as a design strategy for their projects.

Setareh Barimani
B.A. Architecture, 2018

Natya Dharmosetio
B.A. Architecture, 2018

Ernie Theurer
B.A. Architecture, 2018

Faculty Mentor: Jordan Cayanan, Architecture

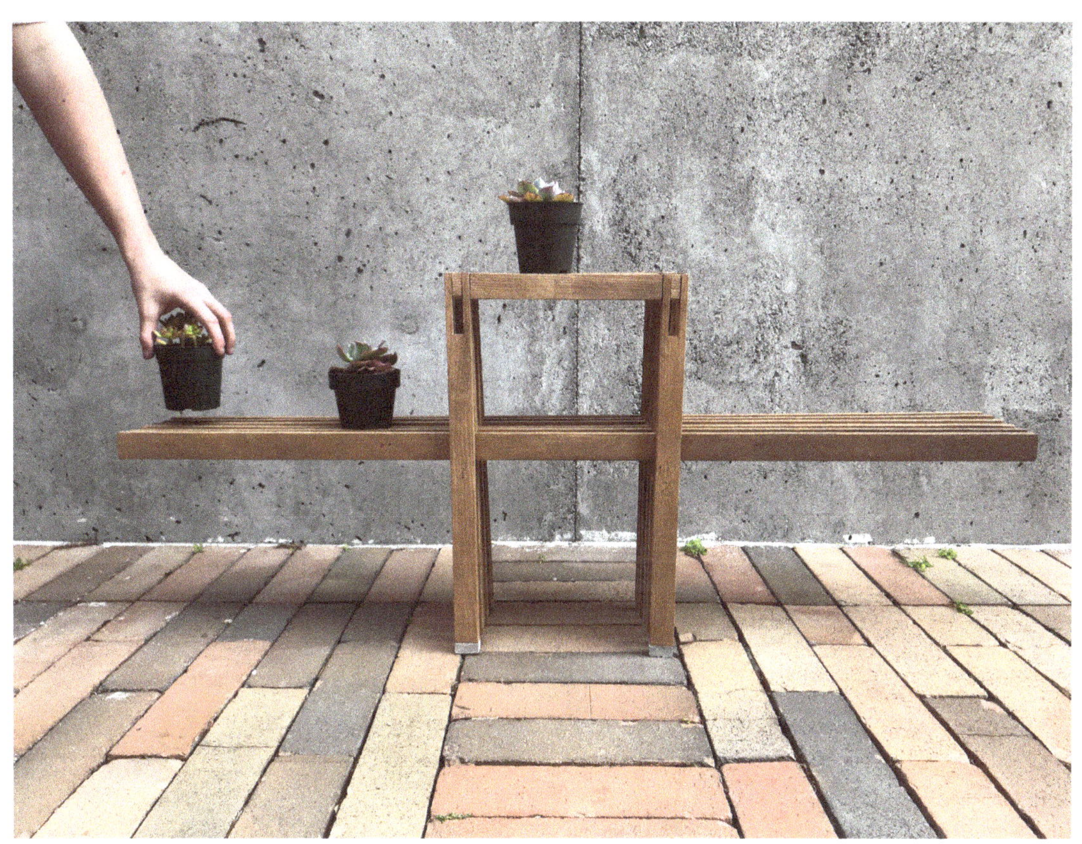

The Wood Planter Project, 2018. Wood.

Yohana Ansari-Thomas

In an homage to Pina Bausch, the performance is composed of several vignettes blending together; they occur simultaneously and separately. People fall in love, they laugh, they struggle, they fight. Chairs are thrown, balloons are popped, walls are scratched, wood is broken. The dancers interact with the environment as a space of flux. The performance describes a certain time of day during which a normally empty space is flooded with liminal interactions. It is on the threshold of many different worlds.

Yohana plays at the crossroad between performance, art, and architecture. His work explores the convention of theatricality and its relationship to space in order to broaden the scope of performative architecture and design. Previous works of his have been selected for CED's Annual Circus. He is originally from Chicago.

Yohana Ansari-Thomas
B.A. Spatial Performance & Design, 2019

Faculty Mentor: Annie Smart, Theater, Dance, and Performance Studies

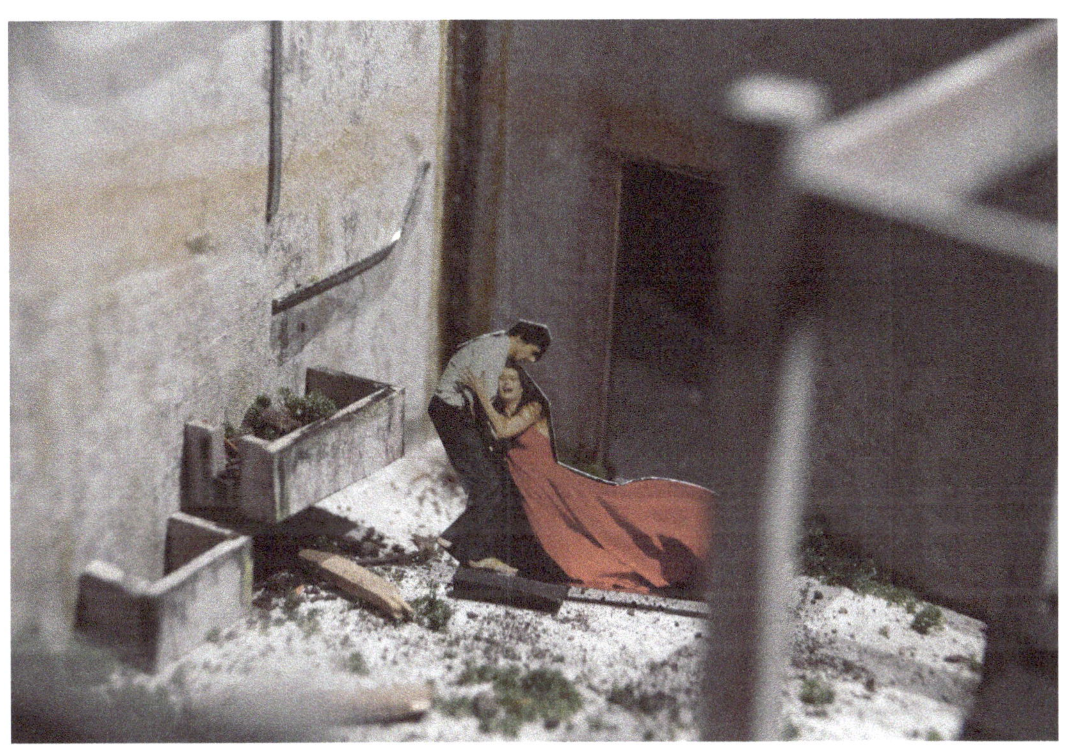

TANZWURSTER, 2018. Scenic design.

GENDER + SEXUALITY

BANK OF HYSTERIA

EYERIS

HARI LEE

MADELEINE CURTIS

NARGES POURSADEQI

SANAZ KHOSRAVI

Bank of Hysteria

In conceptualizing the Bank of Hysteria, we drew from feminist theory and thinkers like Audre Lorde. We played with the idea of offering women, femmes, and gender non-conforming folks "rage receipts" that would serve as a material representation of their anger. The idea of the receipt grew into the metaphor of "investment," ultimately leading us to conceptualize the form of an ATM. In an early conversation about the project, our professor, Jill Miller, used the term "hysterical" in reference to the ways women's anger is commonly dismissed. Bank of Hysteria was not only a feminist pun on a major banking establishment, but a way to connect our project to a larger discourse about the ways women, femmes, and gender non-conforming folks are systematically written off as "too emotional" to be taken seriously.

The team members have backgrounds in computer science, cognitive science, African Diaspora Studies, and Asian American/Asian Diaspora studies, contributing to the project's markedly intersectional implementation. The research that informed this project came from the convergence of all these perspectives, as they pulled from sources in tech, design, psychology, socio-cultural analysis, and black feminism.

Malika Imhotep
Ph.D. African Diaspora Studies

Becca Milman
B.A. Computer Science, 2017

Jessica Liu
B.A. Cognitive Science and Asian
American/Asian Diaspora Studies, 2019

Frances Thai
B.A. Computer Science, 2017

Phyllis Thai
B.A. Interdisciplinary Studies, 2018

Faculty Mentor: Jill Miller, Berkeley Center for New Media

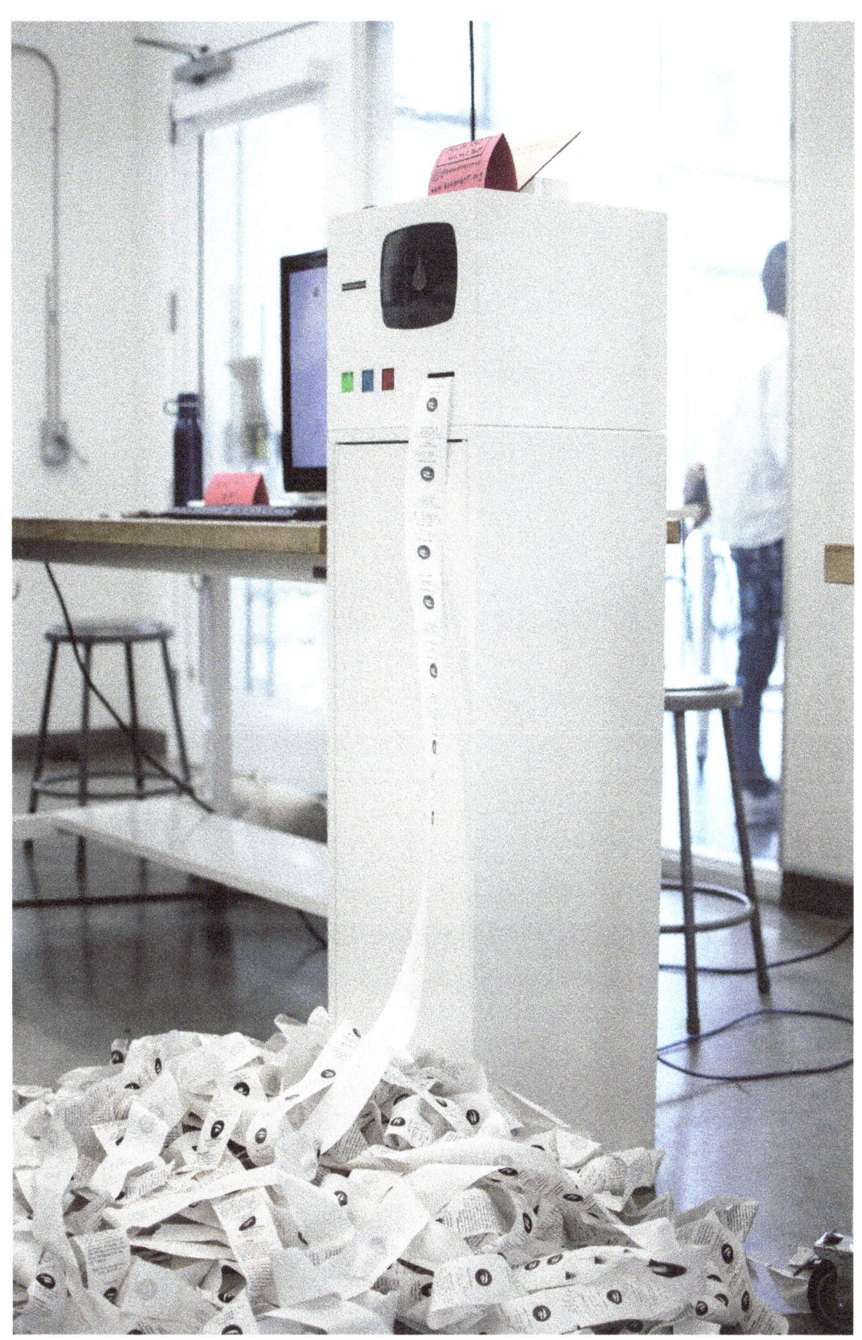

Bank of Hysteria, 2018. Laser cut acrylic, laser-cut wood, Arduino, Raspberry pi, 15 x 15 x 60 in.

Eyeris

Eyeris is a performative wearable that aims to tackle the issue of sexual harassment; specifically, non-consensual touch. It is common for many people, especially women, to experience inappropriate touching in their day-to-day lives. So, how can we prevent these violating encounters from happening? We designed Eyeris: an interactive coat speckled with mechanical irises that deter potential predators from pursuing non-consensual contact. When someone touches the jacket without the wearer's consent, the irises open to reveal eerie, glowing eyes. This causes the assailant to feel like they are being watched, hence discouraging criminal, inappropriate behavior. This subtle yet immediate reaction to touch reminds us to be more cognizant of the implications of our actions.

The Eyeris team is a collaborative crew of four design-minded individuals: George Moore, Silvia Kim, Arianna Ninh and Katherine Qiu. They combined forces for their final project in the course Critical Making. Each shared their unique skills and perspectives over the course of the project's creation: George with his mechanical engineering expertise, Silvia with her soldering savvy and positive energy, Arianna with her attention to detail and craft, and Katherine with her keen time management and assiduity.

Silvia Kim
B.A. Cognitive Science, 2019

Arianna Ninh
B.A. Cognitive Science, 2019

George Moore
Ph.D. Mechanical Engineering, 2021

Katherine Qiu
B.A. Individual Major, 2019

Faculty Mentor: Eric Paulos, Electrical Engineering Computer Science

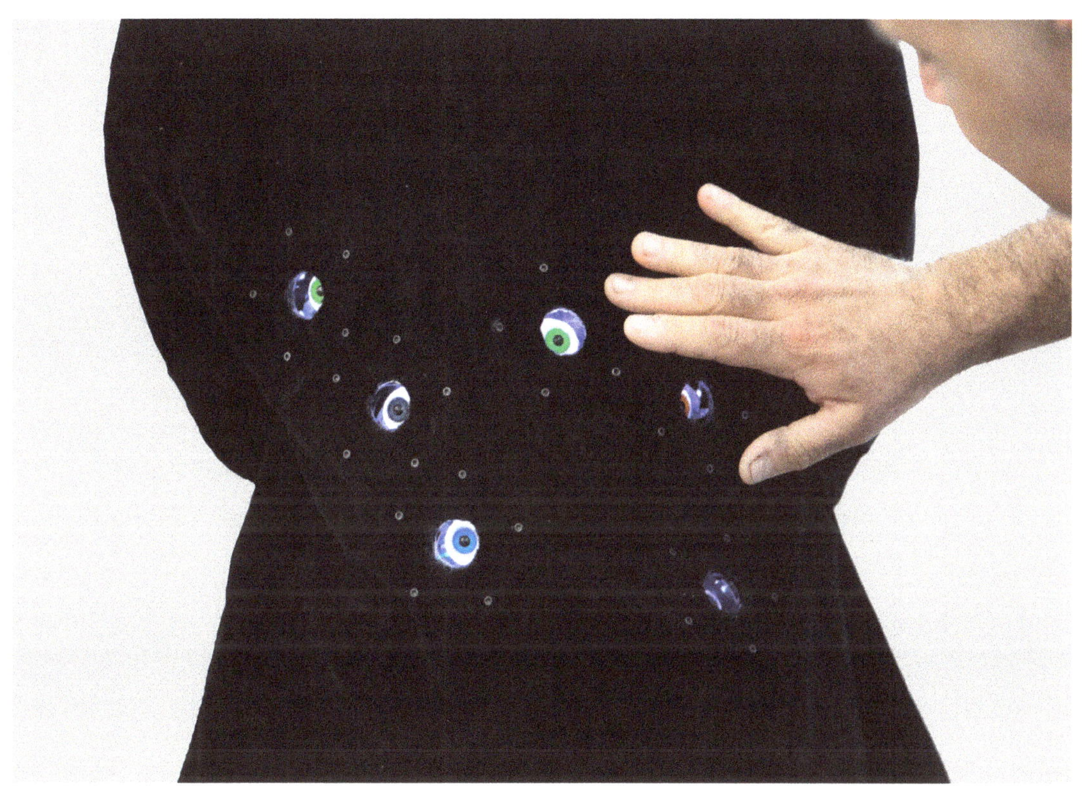

Eyeris, 2018. Vintage velvet blazer, laser-cut acrylic, Arduino, mini servos, wire, bolts, LEDs, plastic eyeballs.

Hari Lee

No Shame in Regression is a collection of poetry portraying the intimacy between a speaker and select others, and the poems flow from depictions of light and simple love to darker feelings associated with love. The choice to avoid capitalization, even for a pronoun like "I," was to convey that no subject in any of the poems was more important than the other. The collection consists of both freestyle poems and poems written in form.

Hari Lee is an undergraduate student at UC Berkeley studying Social Welfare and Child Development. She works part-time at a child development center, and in her free time likes to read and write poetry and play instruments. English is not her first language, but being bilingual helps her appreciate the parts of both English and Korean that are unique to each language.

Hari Lee
B.A. Social Welfare, 2019

Faculty Mentor: Lise Gaston, English

"existence in repentance"

father, look upon us and forgive us for our sins
save your daughters from damnation and show us to light
eyes closed, prayers on lips, hands together, repentance

mother always sheds a tear when she listens
to the story of Christ, bearing our evils, crucified
father, look upon us and forgive us for our sins

boys kissing boys unbeknownst to righteous parents
dirty dreams lead to heartache like a clumsy love bite
eyes closed, prayers on lips, hands together, repentance

letting go of prayers for kisses on lips, on hidden skin
places mother won't see when she bids goodnight
father, look upon us and forgive us for our sins

trying to drown out prayers with lemon and gin
but you can't tune out the voices in your mind
eyes closed, prayers on lips, hands together, repentance

sleeping in motel bathrooms, throwing up in garbage bins
you can't repent when your existence is a vice, but you try
father, look upon us and forgive us for our sins
eyes closed, prayers on lips, hands together, repentance

No Shame in Regression, 2018. Poetry.

Madeleine Curtis

The collection lace & laundry soap *consists of eleven poems that work to explore the complexities of womanhood in the south, touching on the themes of abuse, loss, and motherhood. Emotionally complex adult situations are narrated with a chaotic tone of femininity and recklessness characteristic of a young teenage girl, showcasing the unusual culture around women's issues in a small town in Virginia. The collection explores the cyclical nature of oppression, dissociation, and superstition through the lens of women with hidden narratives who are avoiding their own trauma.*

Madeleine is a student at UC Berkeley with an intended major in Neurobiology and a minor in Creative Writing. In Berkeley, she volunteers at the Humane Society, and at George Mark Children's House in San Leandro caring for inpatient children receiving palliative care. She grew up in Oak Hill, Virginia. This summer, she is working with Remote Area Medical at a mobile clinic in Wise, Virginia. She is also working as a Visiting Scholar at Georgetown University in the medical ethics department. After she graduates, she hopes to attend medical school and eventually study pediatric neurology in combination with rural medicine.

Madeleine Curtis
B.S. Neurobiology, 2021

Faculty Mentor: Lise Gaston, English

"turn ur location on"

paying for chocolate bars in street credit and pink glitter
five doubled over girls dream of snow days rolling away from skin burning blue lights
half barefoot on still hot pavement. formerly on a diet of chewing polaroid pictures
with a side of scraped off freezer ice and baby carrots but now summer is over.
one sits like a safe space with a tooth-crystal and a single high-top nike sneaker
under purple sky it's morning all night and the backroad holds
slow motion car stereo rap under its brick and mortar of cricket noises
in someone's bed she eats pancakes and the cold black metal of a revolver.

boys taking punches for fun don't suffer the trauma
of melting down because they're not split into a pile of file folders calling itself a tree.
a signature of lost shoes and the crushed cereal dust dilemma,
the girls can't be everything the girl can't be.
snapped pink acrylic nails and stolen magic. hit a lick then kiss hard to prevent apraxia.
two go missing. a sugar shattered phone in the street is tracked by the other three.

lace & laundry soap, 2018. Poetry.

Narges Poursadeqi

Marzieh Ebrahim is a young Iranian girl who is a victim of serial acid attacks in Isfahan, Iran. These attacks were carried out by Basij militia under the order of Isfahan's Friday Imam in 2014. They were trying to intimidate women into wearing (what the vigilantes deem) modest dress.

Narges Poursadeqi was born and raised in Tehran, Iran. She started photography and video production at Iranian Youth Cinema Society, and continues studying Fine Art at UC Berkeley. Her work investigates culture, memory, and narrative and how the three oftentimes intersect.

Narges Poursadeqi
B.A. Art Practice, 2018

Faculty Mentor: Brody Reiman, Art Practice

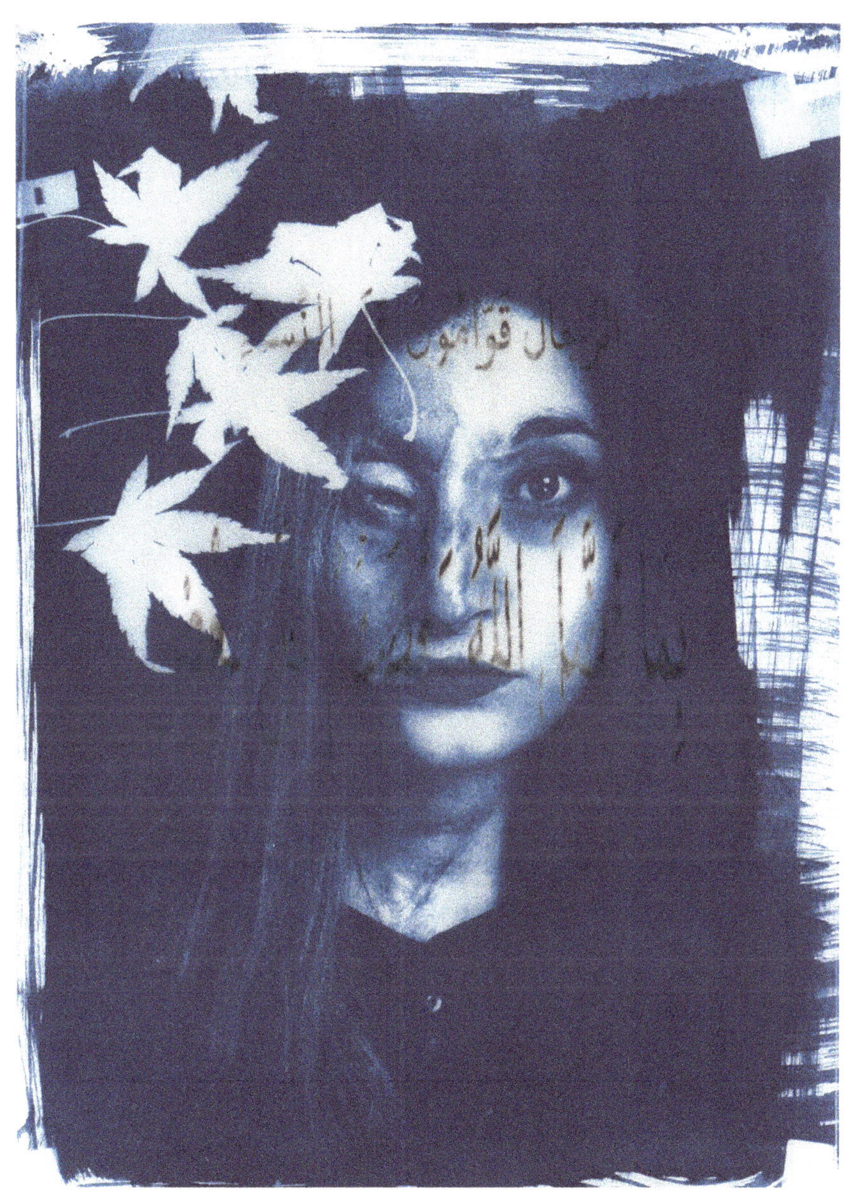

Frozen Light, 2017. Cyanotype on paper, 9 x 12 in.

Sanaz Khosravi

Sometimes the voice we have been searching for in the outside world, can only be heard in the confines of our own being. My work tries to be a reflection of the last battle of darkness and light, the agonizing moments that extend to eternity before succumbing to the dawn. After the Revolution in Iran, compulsory hijab tied the knots that entangled the daily lives of many Iranian women in a cultural struggle where the female hair braided the chains that held her captive to the headscarf.

Sanaz Khosravi was born in Tehran, Iran, in 1990. In 2007, she moved to the United States. Her multimedia art projects have been exhibited across the U.S. and internationally, and most recently at the Berkeley Art Museum and Pacific Film Archive; Craft and Folk Art Museum, Los Angeles; ACCI Gallery, Berkeley; Viewpoint Gallery, Irvine; and Worth Ryder Art Gallery, Berkeley. She is a recipient of Roselyn Schneider Eisner Prizes in Film and Video, Congressional Art Award, Photography Forum Magazine Award of Excellence, President Art Award of DVC, and Design Award of Inspire Oakland Billboard. Sanaz's work aims to create imageries of femininity in the contemporary world. Her works confront social issues while focusing on the concept of hope in daily life.

Sanaz Khosravi
B.A. Art Practice, 2018

Faculty Mentor: Allan deSouza, Art Practice

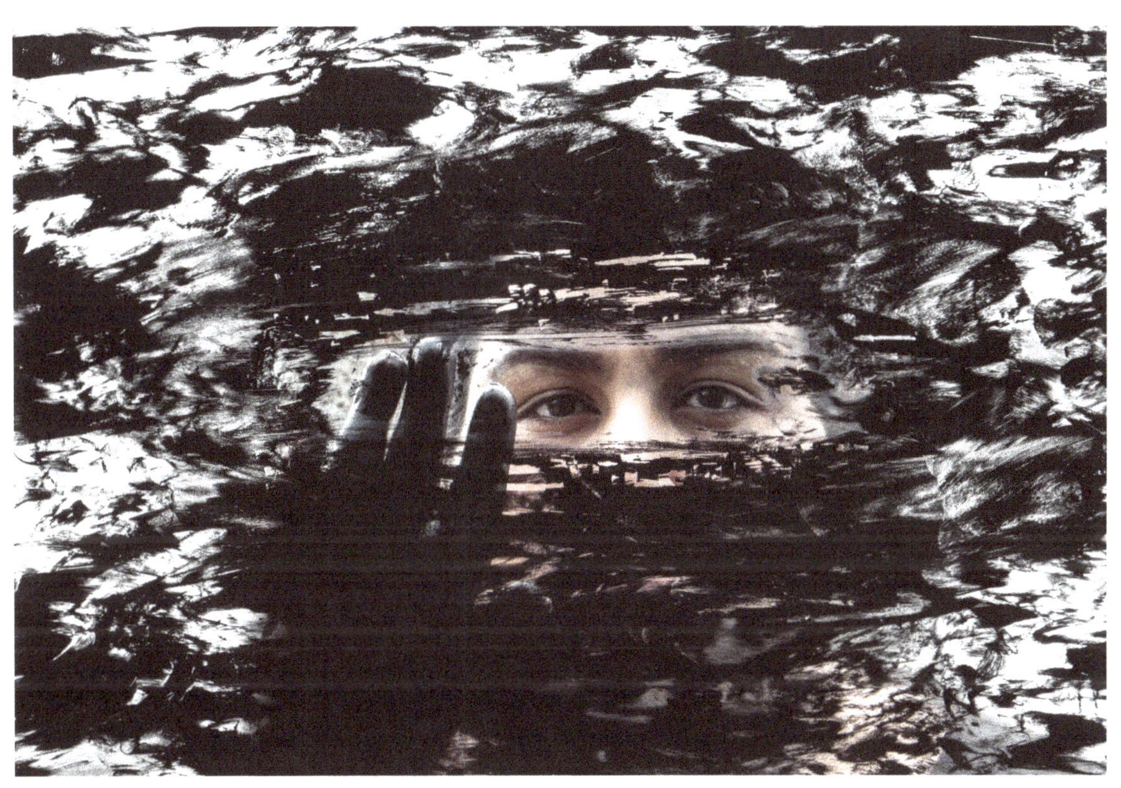

Mirrors, 2016. Gelatin silver print, 30 x 20 in.

GLOBAL CULTURES

AMANDA KACHADOORIAN
DECONSTRUCTING WALLS
LIVIA GOMES DEMARCHI
PATRICK MCBURNIE
SANAZ KHOSRAVI
SERGIO MENDEZ-TORRES

Amanda Kachadoorian

To be placed in a new environment is a way to understand the internal and external aspects of life. I express the notions of identity, psychology, ephemerality, and nature in my work. Every concept has an underlying relationship with one another which is a constant process and investigation. Through the experimentation of mixing various plant life representative of my own multi-cultural background and others, I aim to create the notion of hybridity from a post-colonial identity. While creating an atmosphere of identity through nature, I use a personal motif, "heart in a bowl," which symbolizes effects of displacement, isolation and anxiety. Ephemerality is associated with the constant cycle of life and death in relation to nature and human interaction, which aims to encapsulate a moment that is constantly fleeting. My work aims to create a dynamic atmosphere while providing dialogue surrounding perspectives of individuals and our society.

Amanda Rose Kachadoorian is an emerging Californian artist who was born and raised in San Diego, California. Her art practice has been focused on painting and drawing while experimenting with mixed media, sculpture, and installation. Her body of work aims to express the notions of identity, psychology, ephemerality, and nature. Every concept has an underlying relationship with one another which she intends to create a dialogue around. She derives these ideas from the human anatomy, diverse plant life, and her multi-cultural background.

Amanda Kachadoorian
B.A. Art Practice, 2018

Faculty Mentor: Brody Reiman, Art Practice

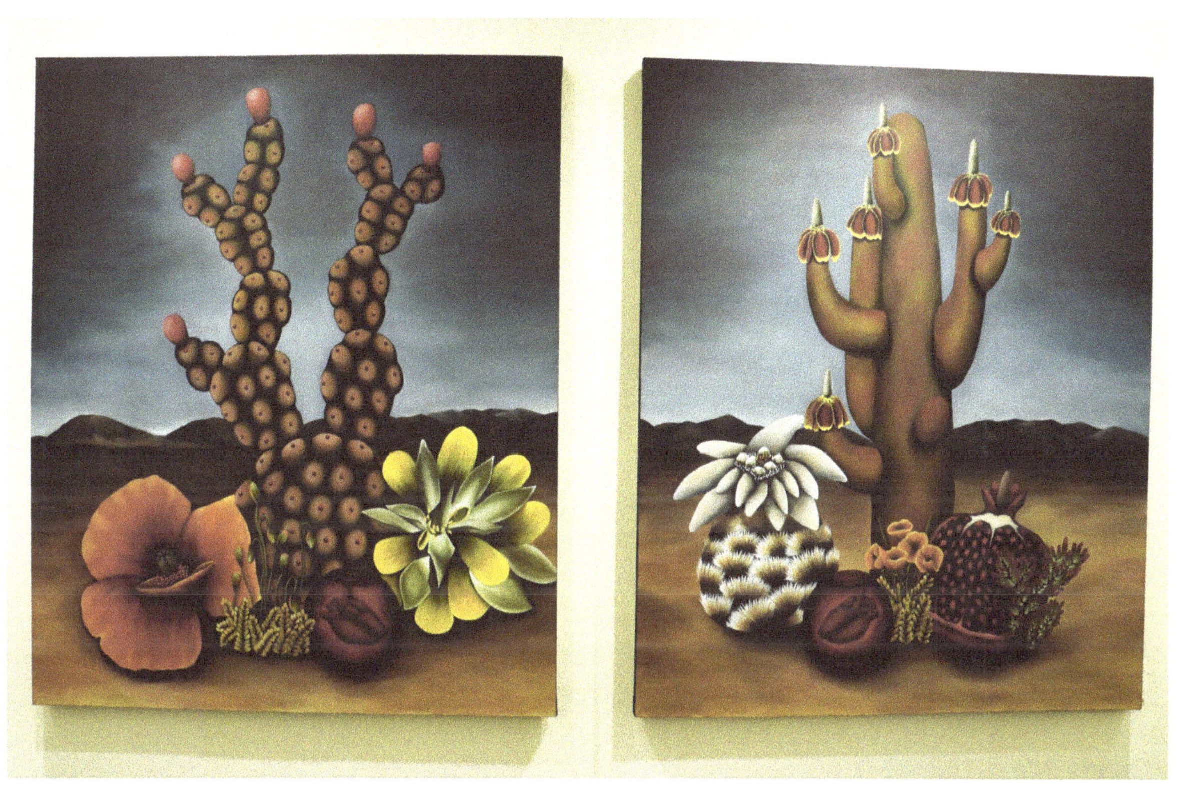

Germexicarian l and Germexicarian ll, 2018. Oil on canvas, 60 x 1 x 72 in.

Deconstructing Walls

The purpose of our provocation is to protest the idea of border walls—both metaphorical and physical—that create violent barriers between immigrants and non-immigrant communities. We designed a model of a brick wall with xenophobic myths about immigrants that were used to propagate support for the building of the U.S.-Mexico border wall engraved on the front side of the bricks. Inside the bricks laid a piece of clear acrylic, on which we engraved data and statistics that negated these myths. Drawing on the concept of deconstruction, the goal of our design is to have audiences interact with the wall by flipping each brick over to the transparent side with the statistics and facts written on them. After each brick is flipped, the wall becomes transparent, creating a powerful metaphor that calls for more education around immigrant issues as we work toward the abolition of these myths and walls.

This team was assembled for the first project of the New Media course, Critical Making.

Purva Juvekar
M.Eng. Mechanical Engineering, 2018

Edward Rivero
LLC Ph.D.

Crystal Lee
B.A. Cognitive Science, 2018

Sally Tran
B.A. Cognitive Science, 2018

Faculty Mentor: Eric Paulos, Electrical Engineering Computer Science; Chris Meyers, Citris and the Banatao Institute

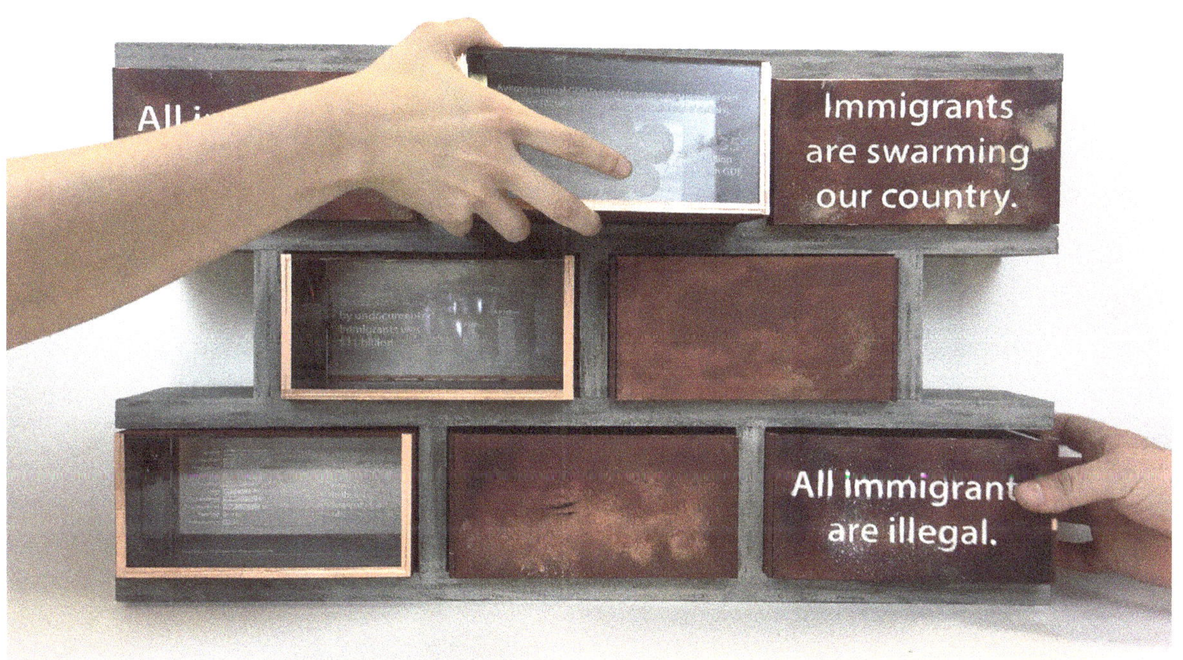

Deconstructing Walls, 2018. Laser-cut wood, acrylic, electronics.

Livia Gomes Demarchi

Quem Eu? *is an autobiographical solo piece about my experience as a young exchange student from the large city of São Paulo, Brazil to rural Kansas in Bush's America. Through humor and critical self-analysis, I explored themes of freedom of speech and cultural microaggressions, questioning the mythos of the "American dream" and whether or not it is accessible to people from other cultures and backgrounds. In the play, I posited the reflection of what this country does to young immigrants and their self-worth when faced with prejudice and xenophobia while healing my personal traumas as a result. I wanted to accentuate the resilience of immigrants, who come to this country with hearts filled with love and hope and deserve an opportunity to pursue their version of the "American dream." With this project, I hoped to honor my cultural roots and continue to open up the dialogue about immigration, not from a statistical point of view, but from within, choosing to retell a painful story through the means of theater and embodied expression.*

Livia Gomes Demarchi is a Bay Area based actor who has performed with companies such as the San Francisco Playhouse (Bengal Tiger at the Baghdad Zoo), *the San Francisco Shakespeare Festival* (Comedy of Errors, Romeo and Juliet, *and* Hamlet), *Marin Shakespeare Company* (Love's Labour's Lost, As You Like It, *and* Richard III), *BRAVA, Crowded Fire, Shotgun Players, Theater Rhinoceros, among others. As an undergrad at UC Berkeley, she expanded on her acting training by exploring other forms of storytelling.* Quem Eu? *marked her playwriting debut. Along with acting projects, she is focusing on Latinx stories and the intersection of social justice with embodied art forms.*

Livia Gomes Demarchi
B.A. Theater and Performance Studies, 2018

Faculty Mentor: Angela Marino, Theater, Dance, and Performance Studies

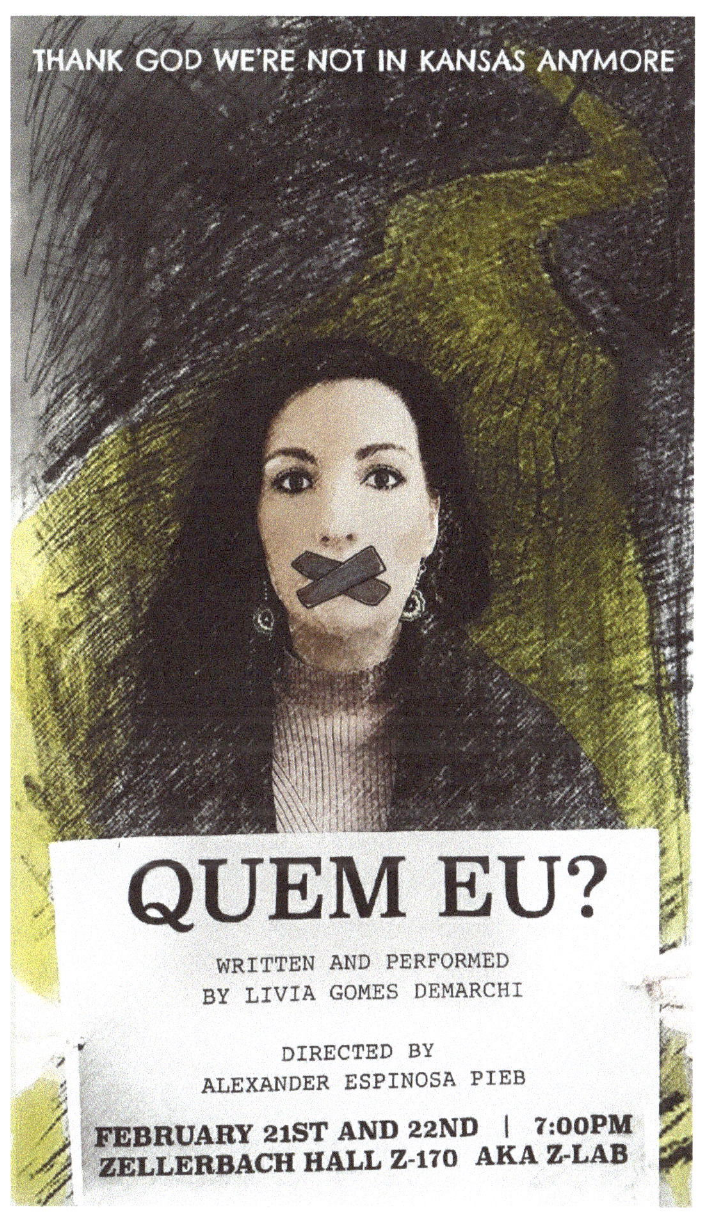

Quem Eu?, 2018. Live performance, 1 hour.

Patrick McBurnie

Lyric Poses is a short collection of six poems centered around the "stances" or personas a writer assumes in the process of composition. The poems are incisive, sassy, and irreverent. Each assumes a different tone and style to convey a range of moods. They blend the personal and the political to comment on the gap between poetry and the world.

Patrick is a poet and writer who is interested in a wide variety of modern arts and literature. He graduated as an English Major in spring 2018.

Patrick McBurnie
B.A. English, 2018

Faculty Mentor: Lyn Hejinian, English; Robert Hass, English

"East and West"

Where does the East end
And the West begin?
Is there a marker there?
(Presumably in the ocean.)
Like a city-welcome sign, reading West.
Population: Jesus Christ,
John Keynes, and George Washington
And on the other side
East. Population: Mao Zedong,
Leon Trotsky, and Krishna the Destroyer
With a small note attached
beneath saying
See reverse
for further details
Or instead of all that
A long dividing line
Like a piece of tape
Stretched across a bedroom floor
Only the bedroom floor is
The ocean floor
And the quarrelsome
Roommates (Picture them
Arguing at the dividing line
of neighboring spaces)
are Mohammed and St. Paul
Or maybe where east and west
Meet each other is marked by
A buoy floating in the water
With a friendly greeter clinging on
Who knows one-hundred-twenty-seven languages
Calling out to whoever passes
In each tongue he possesses
Quicker than an auctioneer
Welcome West! Say Goodday East

Or if the passer-bys are opposite then
Say Goodnight West! Welcome East
I hope that's the case,
And not the alternative:
Tourist infested waters
Surrounded by cruise ships filled with picture-gawkers
Who stand at hollow railings
And stare down into the water
Hoping to glimpse a sign, a greeter, a
Piece of stretch tape floating by
Anything
But they can only see
Their own bovine shadows
Rippling across the surface
Of the blue immensity beneath them

Lyric Poses, fall 2017. Poetry.

Sanaz Khosravi

A Stranger (2017) reflects the existence of the hope in an absolute darkness. It frames paradoxical feelings of being from nowhere and everywhere.

Sanaz Khosravi was born in Tehran, Iran, in 1990. In 2007, she moved to the United States. Sanaz's work aims to create imageries of femininity in the contemporary world and confronts the social issues while focusing on concept of hope in daily life. Her multimedia art projects have been exhibited across the U.S. and internationally, and most recently at the Berkeley Art Museum and Pacific Film Archive, Berkeley; Craft and Folk Art Museum, Los Angeles; ACCI Gallery, Berkeley; Viewpoint Gallery, Irvine; and Worth Ryder Art Gallery, Berkeley. She is a recipient of the UC Berkeley Award of Excellence in Photography, Roselyn Schneider Eisner Prizes in Film and Video, Congressional Art Award, Photography Forum Magazine Award of Excellence, President Art Award of DVC, and Design Award of Inspire Oakland Billboard.

Sanaz Khosravi
B.A. Art Practice, 2018

Faculty Mentor: Azin Seraj, Art Practice

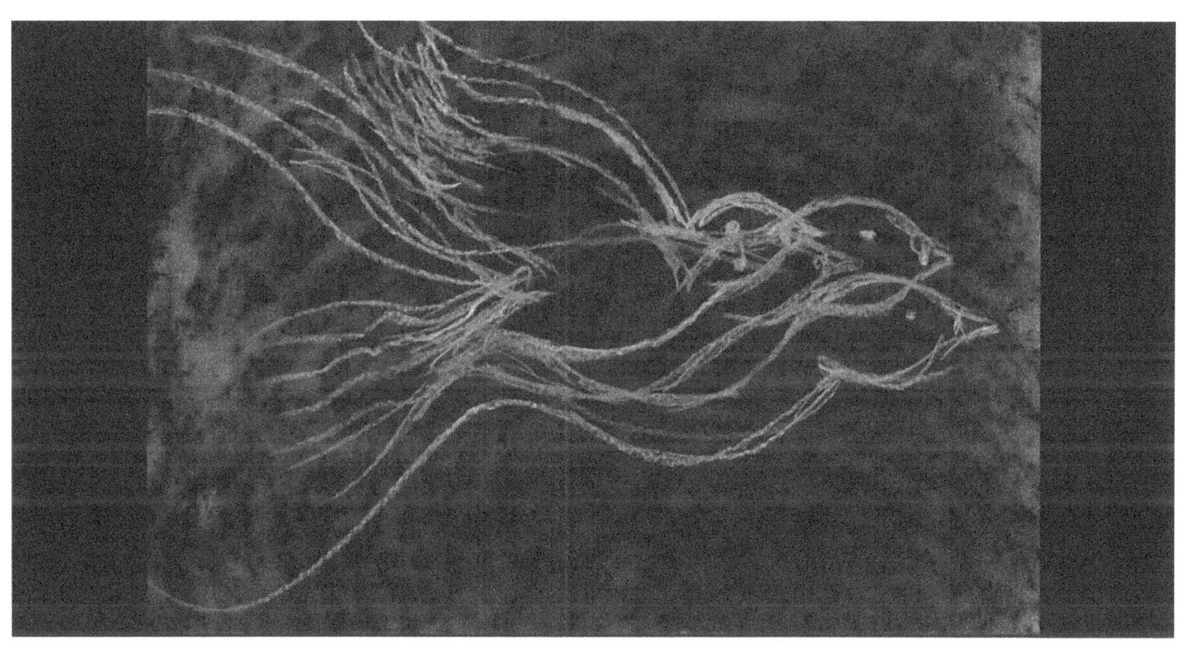

A Stranger, 2017. B&W film, 01:57 minutes.

Sergio Mendez-Torres

Crossing Borders in Order to Make Them Collapse is a short travel narrative that was used as an introduction to my honors thesis. The trip documented was a cross-country train ride to New York City to interview author Ben Lerner and the events that led up to such an opportunity.

Sergio Mendez-Torres immigrated from Mexico to the United States as a young boy. A poet, novelist, photographer, and a recipient of the Robert and Colleen Haas Research Fellowship, Sergio's work explores issues of immigration and self-representation.

Sergio Mendez-Torres
B.A. English, 2018

Faculty Mentor: Lyn Hejinian, English

I sat at the coffee shop, sipping on a dark roast, leg bouncing up and down on the stool, looking over my notes and interview questions, reading over the passages I wanted to cover in *10:04*. I had never conducted an interview, much less of someone well known in the publishing circles of New York City. Understandably, I was nervous.

It was the third hour of my time at this coffee shop, and after watching the coming and going of all types of bodies (both in the shop and the street outside of it), I stood up for a walk.

Fifteen minutes to go. I found myself in some park where no children played. No nannies were present either. There were only men, perhaps working class, perhaps on unemployed, on benches. Some smoked, others read the newspaper. They were all black or Latino. And I, too, sat myself at a bench.

I fiddled with the voice recorder I had purchased for the interview. First the batteries, thentesting for appropriate speaking volume, testing for my familiarity with the settings. I wanted to at least have the appearance of having done this before, of knowing what I was doing. A useful piece of advice I had received from a friend who worked at the local student paper came to mind:

"Sometimes the interview can be as much about the interviewer as the person being interviewed." I thought of Berkeley and my inability to call it home. Did Brooklyn feel more like home? Pigeons hung around my feet, pecking at the concrete in futility. The little jingle from the old Sildenafil citrate commercials I saw on television as a teenager—a jovial little whistle—came into my mind. It was suddenly disrupted by a vibration in my pocket. It was an email from Ben: "I'm here. At the bar. You?" Luckily, I was only a three-minute walk away.

Walter's Restaurant in Fort Greene sits at the corner of DeKalb Ave and Cumberland Street. There was something anachronistic about it, probably being caused by the surrounding boutiques and their storefront remodeling that hid the fact that the architecture was old. I admire Walter's for its authenticity, but also its insistence on not conforming to a certain appearance for marketing purposes.

As I approached the door, a head emerged from out of the restaurant. Two eyes stared at me behind thick-rimmed glasses.

"Are you Sergio?"

"Yes."

A hand extended itself from out behind the half-open door in anticipation of a handshake.

I knew who this was.

"I'm Ben. Nice to meet you."

It was lunchtime and the restaurant didn't offer seating in the booths near the back—only the bars and tables—yet Ben asked if we could have a booth because we were about to conduct an interview and the bar would have been too loud. The host was more than happy to oblige. I wondered if Ben was using some kind of celebrity (or the semblance of it) to break the rules.

As we sat across from one another, Ben said, "So, before you interview me, I want to actually interview you."

I gulped the heavy rock in my throat and shook my head in the affirmative. The sudden feeling of being unprepared came over me.

"Where are you from?"

I proceeded to tell my once-undocumented story. My parents had brought me into this country when I was a toddler, under the guise of another child that had permission to come into the United States. My parents' need to constantly look for better paying work, required we move around a lot, so I had always felt the inability of having a "hometown"—like Topeka, Kansas, for example—quite strongly. I deconstructed the "home" aspect of the word. As an immigrant, there had never, for me, been a place which I inhabited and felt comfortable (happy?) enough to call home. Life had always been moving around in search of another opportunity, in search of another community.

I told Ben about my time as an amateur art photographer in Orange County and how I had to work kitchen jobs to fund my art. I had made the shift from studying photography in community college to studying literature after the positive reception of a poetry and photography zine of my own creation. I knew I wanted to paint with words, to write with photographs, and to have words and image dance around on the same page.

The waiter came over to take our orders, though we hardly had taken a look at the menu. Ben ordered a chicken Caesar salad and I ordered the only vegetarian option on the menu: a fried tomato sandwich with French fries. To be honest, I was a little surprised at the banality of his salad. I was accustomed to Ben ordering eccentric seafood dishes like baby squids and shrimp in puntarelle. To my surprise, I had constructed a sense of Ben Lerner from Ben of *10:04*. Fiction and reality collapsed, but they also had not. The material reality of the situation was that I was in a casual dining restaurant in Brooklyn, sitting with the author of the object of study for my senior thesis, and he was a cool and not-at-all-self-important guy.

What was the author's role in the novel, post-Barthes, where the insistence that the writing process is devoid of the personal intentions and biography of the author? This was a fascinating problem in a new rising genre of the novel, autofiction—a genre which *Leaving the Atocha Station* and *10:04* are often categorized in—where the author was not an avatar, but a persona who may actually have a real-world referent. I was curious about how the rise of this genre came about. What were its political motivations? To challenge. To parody. To disrupt.

"Tell me more about your project," Ben continued, "what got you into it?"

"Well, for a long time, I've had this fascination with writing and the process surrounding it. I've always written creative pieces in the background of my academics and I consider myself very much an artist—if this is not at all pompous to say."

Ben shook his head in the negative as hands came to refill our water glasses.

"Metafiction," I went on, "draws me in because it brings the making of the art to the forefront. It doesn't pretend to be anything other than what it is. It throws the impossible asymptotic attempt of realism out the window, in favor of allowing the reader access to the behind-the-scenes stuff that one would not normally read otherwise when they pick up a, say, Dickens novel. I read *10:04* as a metafiction."

Ben's eyebrows raised up, so I panicked that I must have said something wrong.

"Wait, Ben, did I say the title correctly? Ten-o-four? Or, is it ten-four?"

He shrugged and said, "Sure."

The waiter arrived with our food, stringy French fries nearly spilling off of my plate. An entire chicken breast with nearly-perfect grill marks laid on top of Ben's salad, cut into eight different pieces. Have you ever wondered how other people eat? Usually, most of us don't pay any mind to this, outside of certain people that studiously stare at the jaw to see how it moves in often barbaric ways. Given the celebrity I felt surrounded Ben, I couldn't help the curiosity looming over how he ate. Would he chew with his mouth open? Talk with his mouth full of food? Make strange whimpering noises of delight after swallowing? I seemed to be having a desire to break down the writer before me into habits and quirks. What was this fetish that I felt?

"Do you write poetry or fiction?" Ben asked.

"Both, actually. In fact, that's what fascinated me about your two novels, that switch from poetry to fiction. To me, that felt like something refreshing for the novel right now. Aren't most literary novels published right now from people with MFAs? How does the novel, as a genre, not then congeal towards a variation on the same thing someone else is already doing?"

Ben raised his eyebrows again and I panicked again.

"I mean, not that there is anything wrong with having an MFA. I want an MFA, as well. It's just an observation. For someone that wants to publish one day, it seems like the move to make is to head to an MFA program. I'm just wondering if having a sphere populated—I hesitate to say saturated, though I want to—with people who learned craft programmatically, won't everyone eventually just sound the same?"

"Well, yeah, I don't think that's wrong. I don't read a lot of contemporary fiction right now because I find a lot of it incredibly boring, as if I am reading a sitcom."

We both chuckled. Behind Ben's head, I could see a small child jumping up and down on her booster seat as her mother tried to spoon feed her what appeared to be chicken noodle soup.

"I partly blame the Y.A. novel for that and the overwhelming melodrama that surrounds it," I said.

A pattern was established as Ben raised his eyebrows once more and I reacted with panic. Was my comment too flippant?

"What would you get your creative writing MFA in? Poetry or fiction?"

"I find that question incredibly difficult to answer. On the one hand, I really love telling stories? But on the other, I've written more poems than anything else. Why can't I do both? Why do I have to only focus on one thing? Anne Carson, Sylvia Plath, and Gertrude Stein didn't focus on one genre of writing and I admire their work a lot. I just don't see why we need to distinguish poet, essayist, and novelist from one another. Aren't they all writers?"

"I think it has to do with focus more than anything. A lot of the people that you will be mentored under will only have written in one of those categories. But I don't think you're wrong in wanting to write a little bit of everything either."

"Thank you. I guess if I had a gun-to-my-head scenario, I would pick fiction."

"Why?"

"Because I already feel like a poet, despite never having a collection of poems, or even a single poem published. Poetry comes naturally to me, as strange as that may sound."

I tried not to stare at Ben's mouth as he chewed. Scraping the last bit of ketchup from my plate with a few fries, I continued speaking, so as to shift the focus away from myself.

"This all reminds me of one of the early interviews of the *Paris Review*. The Faulkner one, specifically. Have you ever read it?"

"I'm not sure. Perhaps not."

"Well, the main thing to that is that Faulkner makes this claim that always stuck with me, which is that every novelist and short story writer wants to be a poet. He said that those who get into writing fiction are actually failed poets. I'm paraphrasing, of course."

"That's interesting. I'll have to read that interview."

"Speaking of interviews, maybe we could switch to yours?"

Excerpt from *Crossing Borders in Order to Make Them Collapse*, 2018. Creative nonfiction.

HEALTH

Artists in Residents

Artists in Residents (AiR) is an initiative of the Suitcase Clinic, a weekly student-run organization that has been serving Berkeley's homeless community for over 30 years. In response to the mental health needs of this population, AiR seeks to provide arts and music programming within clinic spaces while leveraging the Suitcase Clinic's unique ability to elevate and advocate for unhoused Berkeley residents. The team will partner with local art therapy organizations and social workers to implement art and music workshops, galleries, and performances. AiR will provide creative outlets for self-expression, promote mental health, and foster self-efficacy and upward mobility. Over one year, AiR will work with 30-50 individuals to provide safe spaces to practice, develop, and showcase their artistic talents.

AiR is a team of five undergraduate volunteers who have been working for and within the Suitcase Clinic throughout their college careers. Using their own unique creative passions, they hope to create a new dimension of community within the Clinic spaces that we have come to know and love. In the process, they hope to grow further with participants in empowering and advocating around homelessness and basic needs security.

Kyle Gibson
B.A. Public Health, 2019

Monica Schreiber
B.A. Public Health, 2019

Mark Houdi
B.A. Molecular & Cell Biology, 2019

Rasika Sudharshan
B.A. Cognitive Science and Molecular & Cell Biology, 2019

Krupa Modi
B.A. Public Health, 2019

Allie Yip
B.A. Integrative Biology, 2019

Faculty Mentor: Phillip Denny, Big Ideas Team

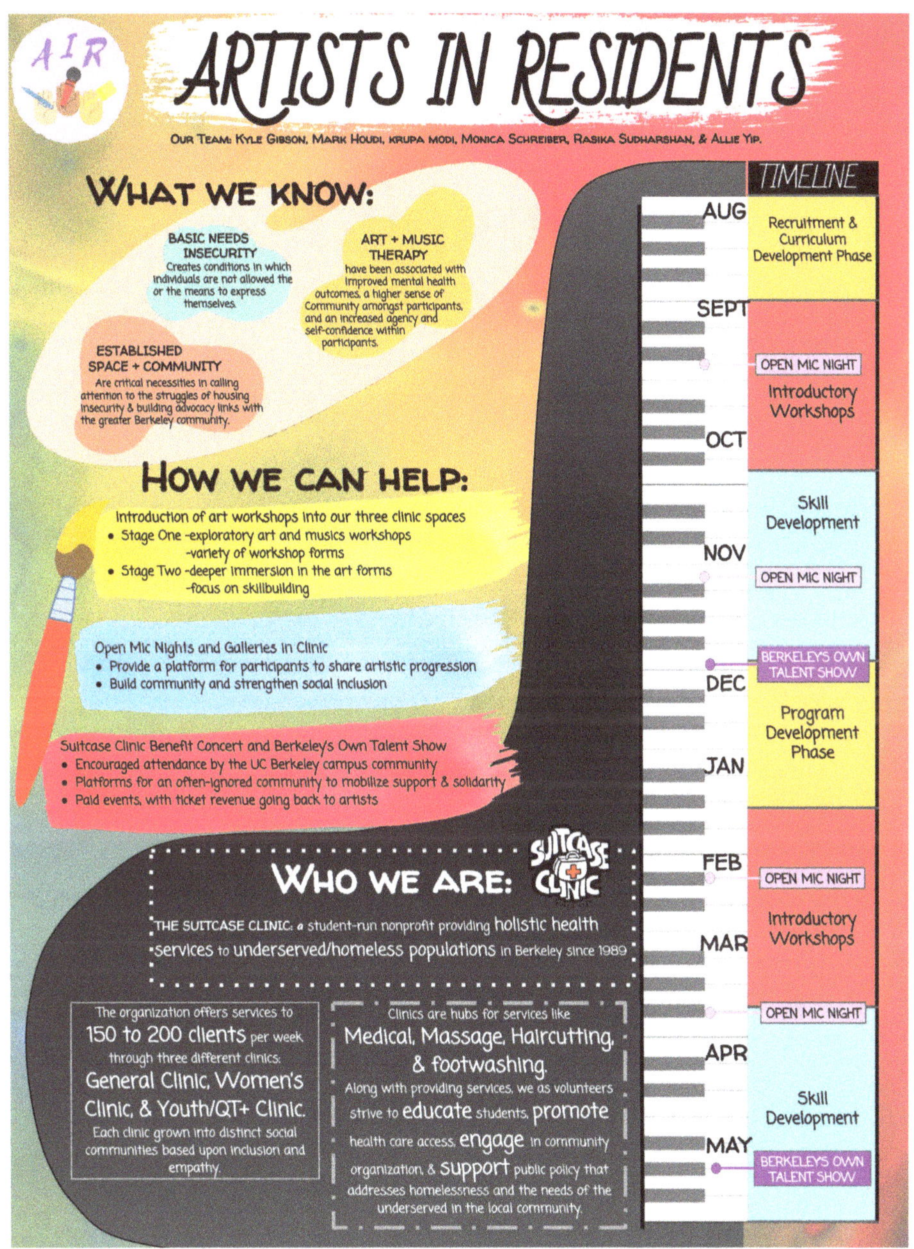

Artists in Residents, August 2018 - May 2019. Live performance, multimedia visual artworks, Variable time.

Bonafide

We do not match make; people find their own dates, and then they can choose to do our box/activity to slow down and humanize the dating process. This will allow the two people to get to know each other better. In this era of technology, dating can be fast-paced and shallow. The process involves two people matching online or finding each other in real life. First, they decide to buy a set of Bonafide boxes to get to know each other better, next they take a week to fill out the boxes to represent their lives (through answering insight questions and drawing prompts, as well as explaining their memories), then they get together and discuss the contents of the box.

The Bonafide team is a group of User Experience Designers that come from varying design and technical backgrounds. They found that facilitating a relationship is completely varied, and individuals often tend to use varied platforms. However, a key takeaway they were able to build upon was that when individuals have already met another a viable partner or even a potential friend, there is often an initial sense of awkwardness that prevents true meaningful conversations from the get-go. Thus, they aimed to work in this space to help create meaningful first conversations.

Daniel Chang
B.A. Economics, 2018

Sarah Malone
B.A. Cognitive Science, 2020

Ji Soo Kim
B.A. Cognitive Science, 2018

Ivy Nguyen
B.A. Computer Science, 2020

Priyanka Saiprasad
B.A. Cognitive Science and Data Science, 2020

Faculty Mentor: James Pierce, School of Information;
Claire Dunnington, Haas School of Business

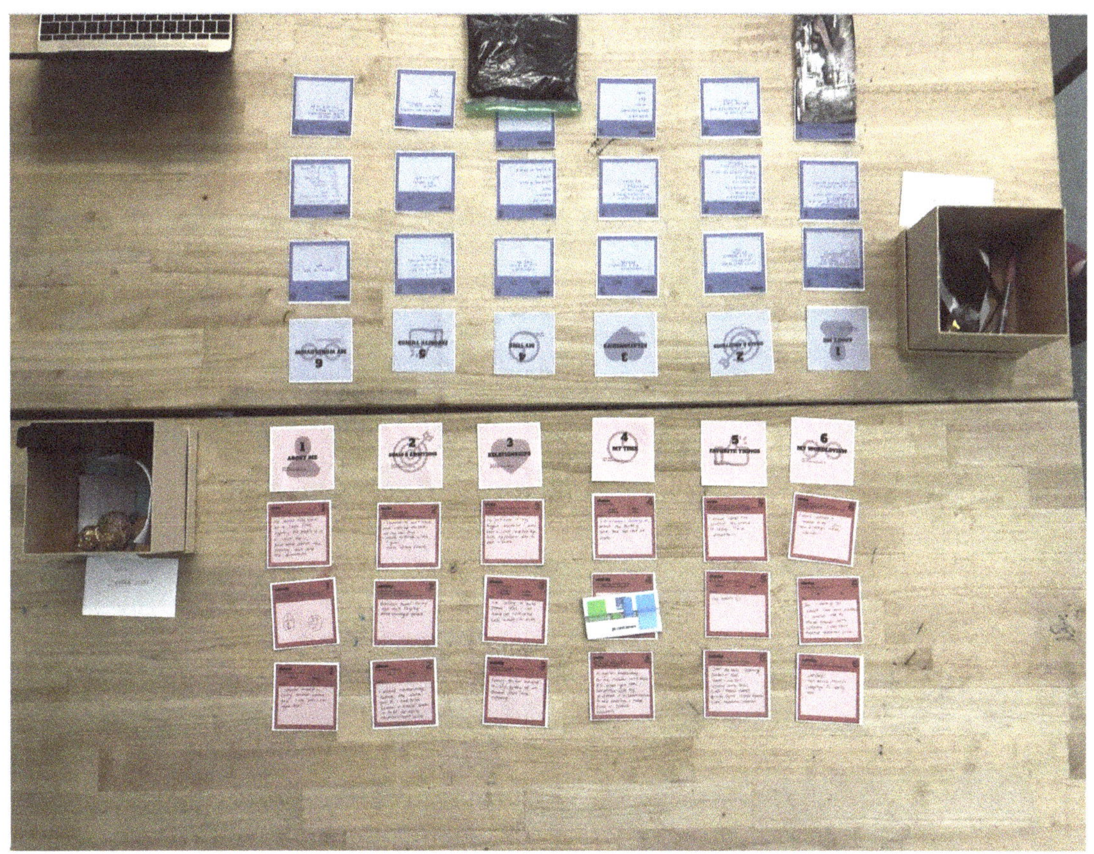

Bonafide, spring 2018. Physical Prototyping, cardboard, cardstock, and digital UI/UX, Variable dimensions.

Hazanne (Sidney) Likwong

Imprint is a self portrait project I had done for my art class. This project involves depicting the self in our own creative representations. It is my first try at animation. It illustrates my struggle with the inner demons that I have encountered since childhood. We can see the demon haunting the subject, but ultimately the protagonists learns to accept and live with it.

Sidney has loved and has been making art since she was young. She has always dreamed of being an influential artist that can inspire change or motivate others to create art as well.

Hazanne (Sidney) Likwong
B.A. Art Practice and Urban Studies, 2019

Faculty Mentor: Maggie Lawson, Art Practice

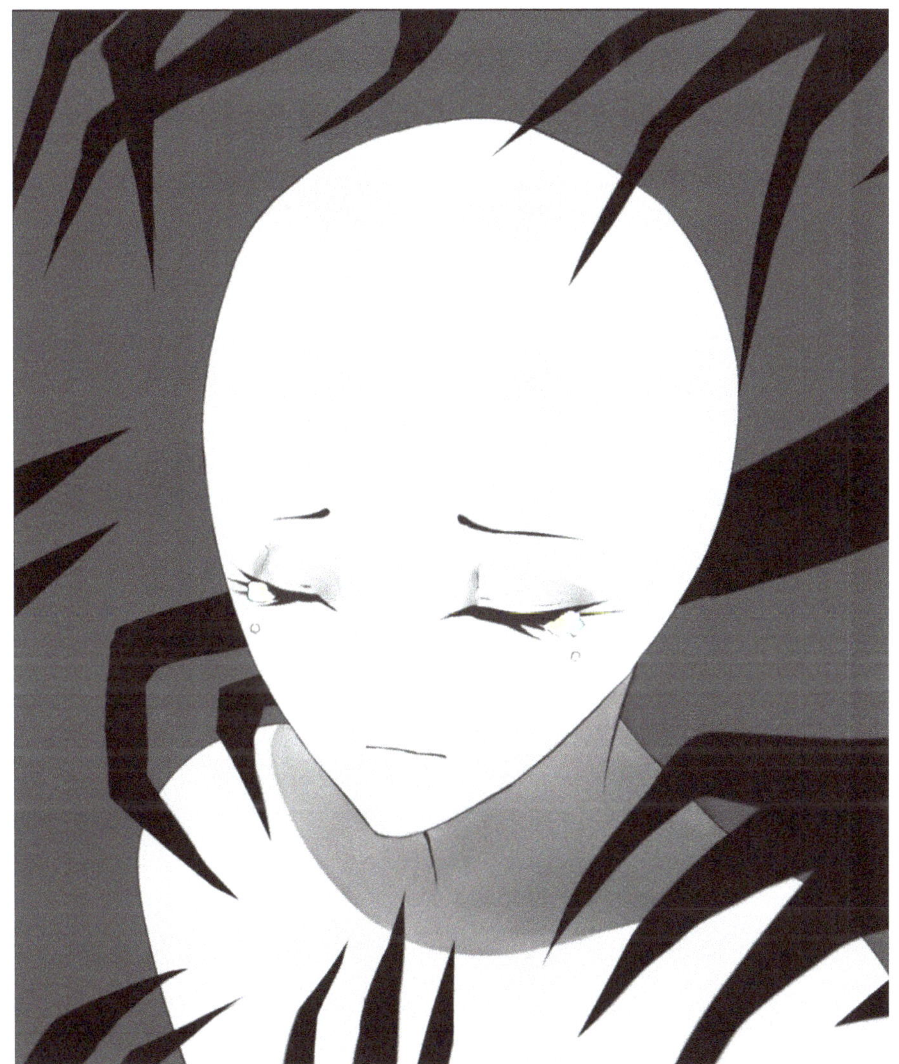

Imprint, 2018. Digital animation, 0:54 seconds.

PerSpectacles

Many of today's problems stem from social disconnect, despite social media's promise of making the world more "connected." That is why we created PerSpectacles, a pair of spectacles that challenges the promise of a more connected world. They provide a comfortable, but narrowed perspective, symbolic of the actual effect social media has on our world view. Each of the lenses was designed to exaggerate the ways in which technology facilitates and/or manipulates the way we view the world (e.g. unduly optimistic, narrow-minded, and ignorant). The ability to manually control the filters, as users of technology, is symbolic of our role in causing our lives to become more filtered, controlled, and detached.

Team PerSpectacles is composed of four students at UC Berkeley who share an interest in design, despite the differences in their years and majors. The team formed for an assignment in their Critical Making class where the prompt was to build a wearable. Motivated by their shared experiences in college, the team decided to use the project to address the issue of how social media filters life, causing feelings of social disconnect.

Nour Eldifrawy
B.S. Materials Science and Engineering, 2018

Crystal Lee
B.A. Cognitive Science, 2018

Nigel Mevana
B.S. Mechanical Engineering, 2018

Leeann Hu
B.A. Molecular & Cell Biology, 2019

Faculty Mentor: Eric Paulos, Electrical Engineering Computer Science

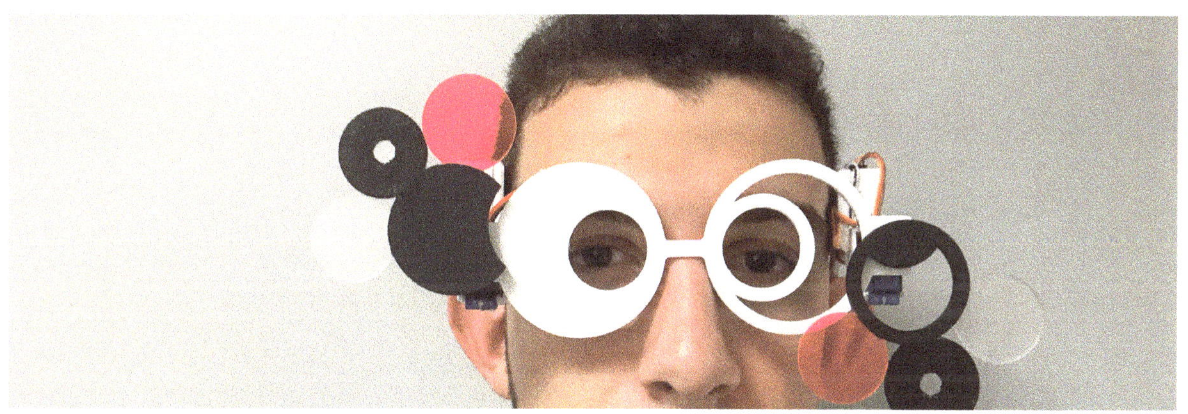

PerSpectacles, 2018. 3D printing and electronics, 4.75 x 6.25 x 2.85 in.

Rae Maxwell-Ross

Statistics is part of a larger project of collecting and archiving the real life stories of those affected by mental illness. These stories then become the inspiration for the large scale interactive installations wherein the recorded stories are shared. To contribute to the collection or find more stories, please visit beyondstatistics.weebly.com online.

Rae Maxwell-Ross (RMR) is a Bay Area artist who works in a wide variety of media, including film, installation, and printmaking. Drawing on her own lived experiences of anxiety and deeply affected by a family history of mental illness, her work explores such themes as grief, stigma, and denial.

Rae Maxwell-Ross
B.A. Art Practice, 2018

Faculty Mentor: Brody Reiman, Art Practice

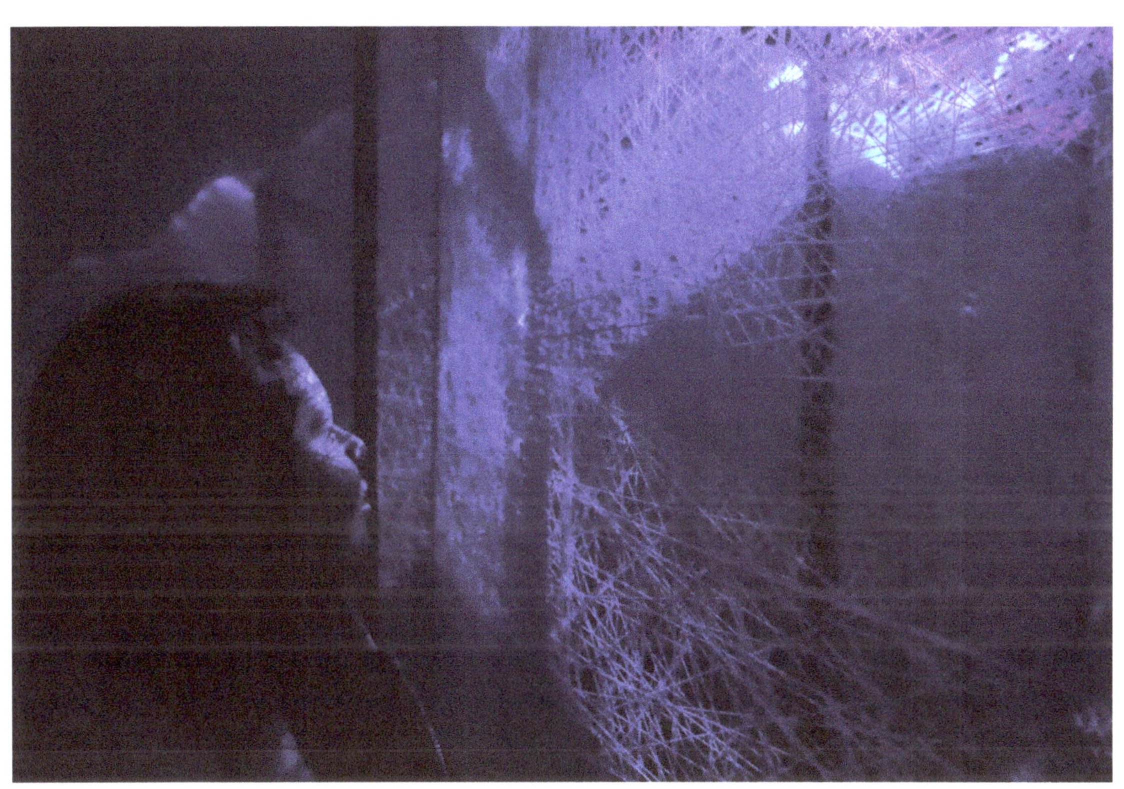

Statistics, 2017 – Present. Audio installation, Variable dimensions.

Smart Can

The Smart Can empowers lifeguards to focus on their most critical jobs—saving lives!—by autonomously collecting and aggregating ocean rescue data in real-time. Though it is hard to believe in this hyper-connected day and age, lifeguards are currently expected to hand-record all information following each and every rescue occasion. To remove the burden of collecting rescue data from lifeguards, we have equipped the standard Burnside buoy ("can"), a device uniformly relied upon by lifeguards to tow swimmers to safety, with the ability to automatically send a signal and record data every time a rescue occurs. Our Smart Can is augmented with capacitive sensors on both handles along with a water sensor, which—when activated simultaneously, meaning that a rescue is in progress—communicate with the lifeguard tower through WiFi.

Team Smart Can worked to meaningfully integrate "a simple human-powered transportation technology with a novel interactive experience." Because one team member is involved in the lifeguarding community and had experienced pain points firsthand, the team quickly realized they wanted to explore bringing the 50-year-old Burnside buoy—colloquially known as the "can"—into the digital age.

Fiona Duerr
B.A. Urban Studies, 2018

Purva Juvekar
M.Eng. Mechanical Engineering, 2018

Nour Eldien Eldifrawy
B.S. Materials Science & Engineering, 2018

Christina Pappas
MBA, 2018

Faculty Mentor: Eric Paulos, Electrical Engineering Computer Science

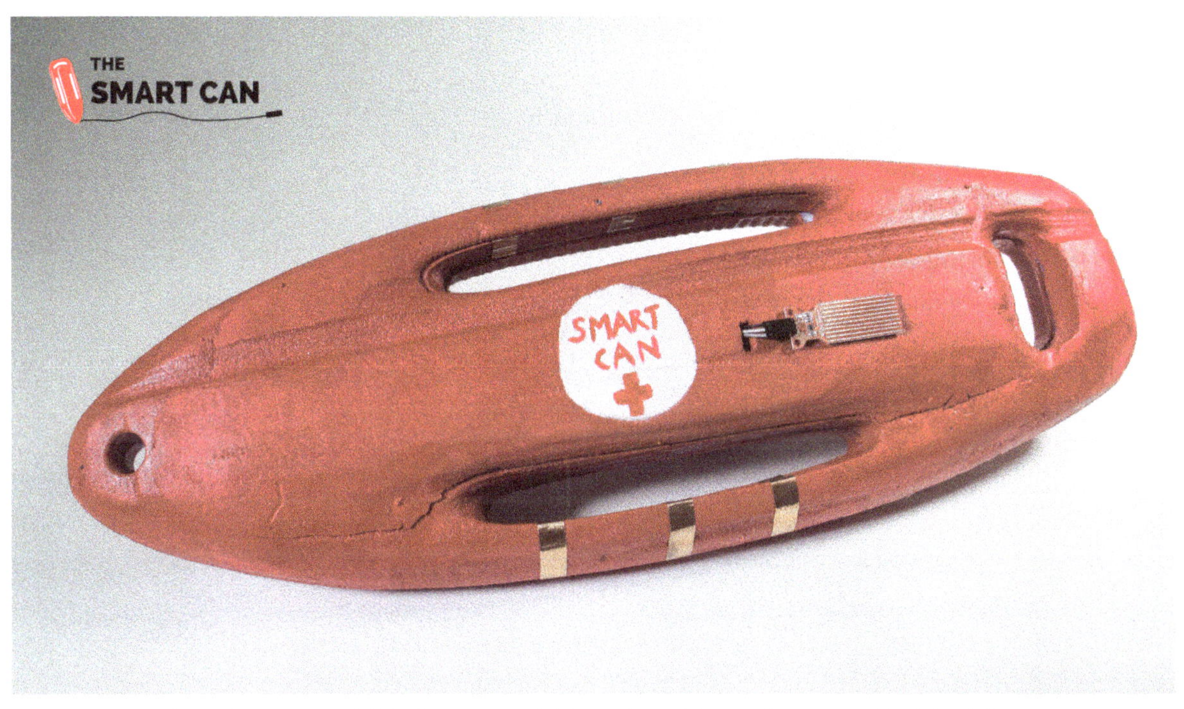

Smart Can, spring 2018. Prototype, CNC-machined foam, electronics, 7 x 21 x 3.5 in.

Tearrarium

Tearrarium is a tear-activated therapy garden that uses tear sensing technology to transform your tears into new life. By putting on the pair of glasses and having yourself a good cry, your tears will activate an internal irrigation system to water and grow your plants. Tearrarium allows for a restorative experience by exposing users to nature's healing powers while encouraging them to tend to their own emotional garden. As a performative piece, our design combines wearable technology and basic principles of ecotherapy to formulate a critique on the social stigma associated with mental health and crying through a critical lens.

The Tearrarium *team consists of five powerful women who all brought unique skills and perspectives to the project. Seiyoung Jang, a technician specializing in musical machines, brought her expertise to the mechanisms working behind the scenes. Crystal Lee, a talented maker and artist, made* Tearrarium *come to life. Arianna Ninh, with her attention to detail and DIY mentality, made sure everything was effortlessly connected. Lieyah Dagan, a critical and aesthetic queen, made sure each piece worked together both visually and symbolically. Fiona Duerr, a creative working at the intersection of art and science, contributed highly to ideation and additionally oversaw the build.*

Lieyah Dagan
B.A. Design for Urban Life, 2018

Seiyoung Jang
M.F.A. Electronic Music & Recording Media,
Mills College Department of Music, 2018

Fiona Duerr
B.A. Urban Studies, 2018

Crystal Lee
B.A. Cognitive Science, 2018

Arianna Ninh
B.A. Cognitive Science, 2019

Faculty Mentor: Jill Miller, Berkeley Center for New Media
Faculty Mentor: Eric Paulos, Electrical Engineering Computer Science

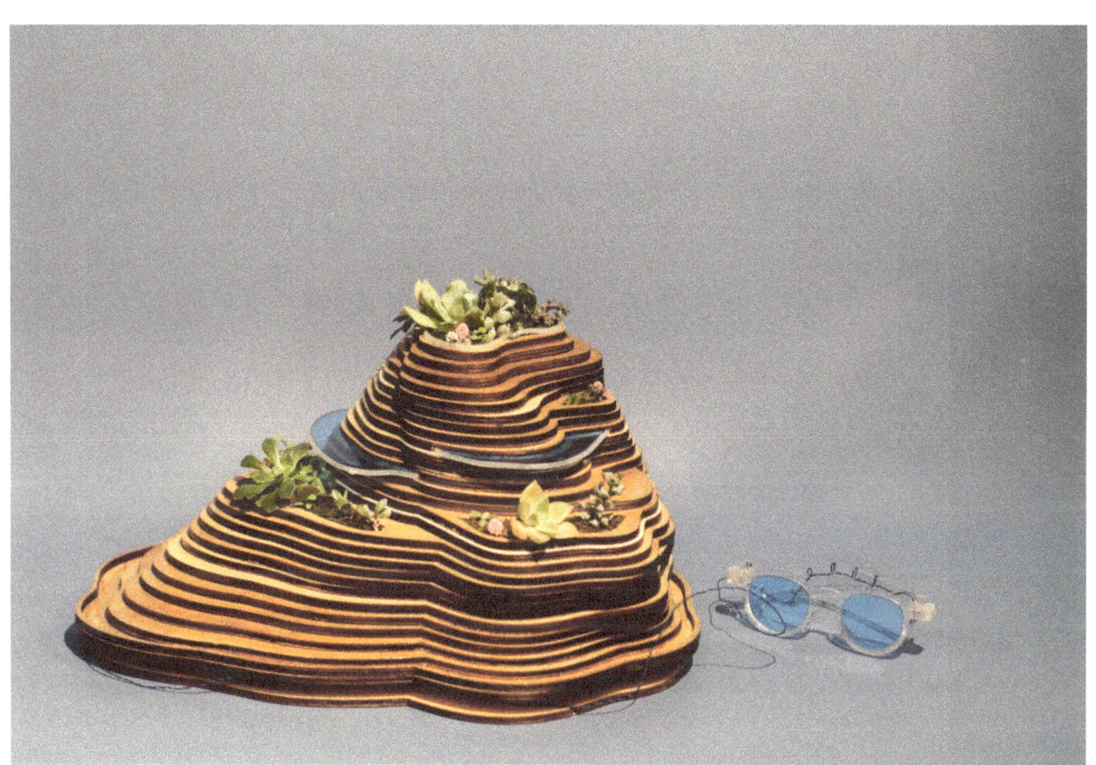

Tearrarium, 2017. Laser-cut wood, laser-cut acrylic, copper tape, succulents arduino, artificial or real tears, peristaltic pump. 17 x 14 x 9 in.

Universal Socket Prosthetic

The Universal Socket Prosthetic is an affordable, accessible, and customizable solution to hand prosthetics for people of all ages. While most prosthetic hands can cost thousands of dollars, our design allows anyone with access to a 3D printer to create their own prosthetics at a fraction of the cost without sacrificing functionality. The design features a base socket that attaches to the arm, including hexagonal gaps for increased flexibility, breathability, and aesthetic appeal, creating a product that any user can feel comfortable using. With the simple yet effective hex-lock attachment design on the base, the user will be able to switch between different attachments depending on the task they are trying to accomplish within seconds.

Team DASH consists of four members, Dominic, Akhi, Stephen, and Hunter. They all come from diverse backgrounds, including mechanical, bio, and civil engineering, which has helped them come together to create a product none of them could achieve on their own. Though the team members come from different disciplines, they share the common interests of human-centered design, improving the way users live their lives, and inspiring innovation in other designers.

Dominic Chiavacci
B.S. Bioengineering, 2018

Akhilesh Mishra
B.S. Mechanical Engineering, 2018

Hunter Garnier
B.S. Mechanical Engineering, 2018

Stephen Shelnut
B.S. Civil Engineering, 2019

Faculty Mentor: Grace O'Connell, Mechanical Engineering

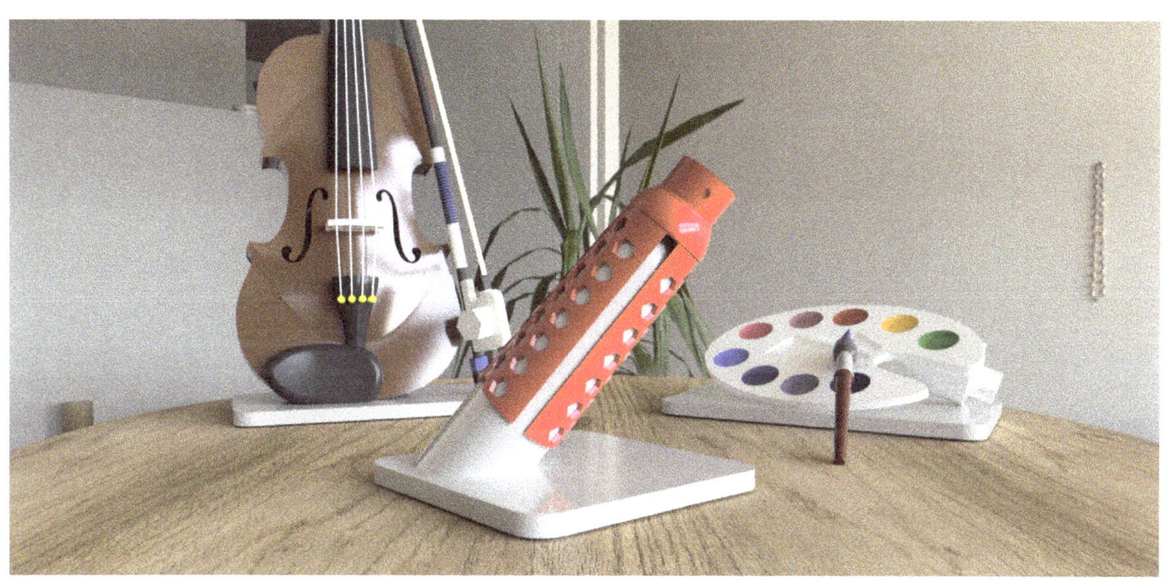

Universal Socket Prosthetic, 2017. 3D printing, 10 x 10 x 30 cm.

SPIRITUALITY

MELISSA CHAPMAN
REED JONES
YUAN ZHUANG

Melissa Chapman

Meta Morphic starts with sunrise colors lighting ten river rocks placed neatly all around the stage. Moments later, nine dancers and I appear on the upstage left corner. Ahead of us lies a rock bed that surrounds a pool of still water—soon to be broken by a stream of water from above. What followed was an experimental conversation between ourselves and the elements, involving physicality and vocalizations that took us on a journey towards that alluring waterfall. Earth, air, fire, and water instigated and inspired our movements and our words, and called on us to dare to be strong, to discover, and to listen closely to each other.

Born in Monterey, California and raised in the rainforests of Costa Rica, Melissa Chapman never dreamed she would be in the graduating class of 2018. Nine other dancers and fellow UC Berkeley students helped bring Meta Morphic to life last spring. Their names: Hope Fellows, Amainary Contreras, Bruna Gill, Crystal Chan, Danitza Mariana Morante, Elizabeth Scarlett, Kathy Liu, Stella Caroline Ji and Victoria Marie; many of them are also graduating this spring 2018 semester.

Melissa Chapman
B.A. Theater and Performance Studies; Minor in Dance and Performance Studies

Faculty Mentor: James Graham, Theater, Dance, and Performance Studies

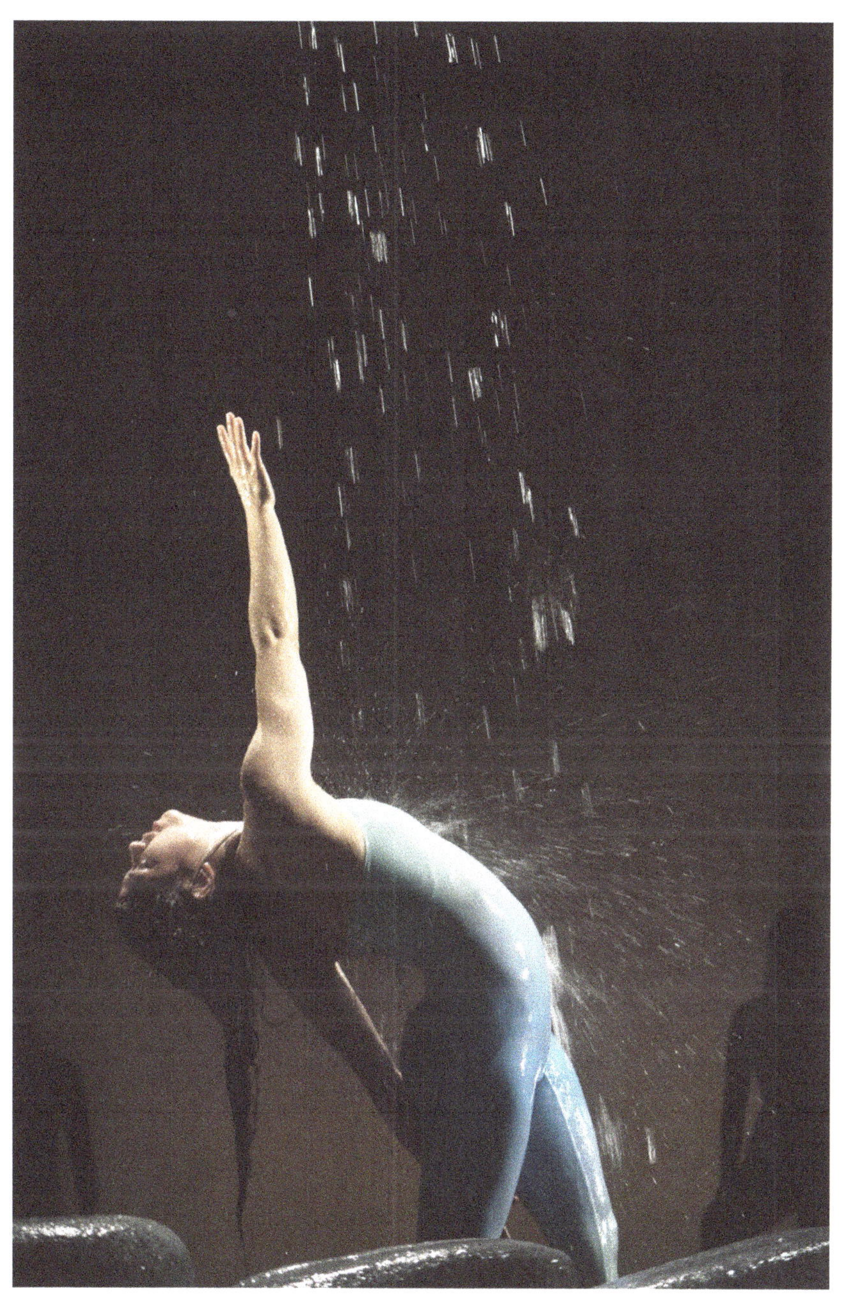

Meta Morphic, spring 2017. Live performance, 26 minutes.

Reed
Jones

In Mary Zimmerman's Tony Award nominated play, Metamorphoses, *the classical tales of Ovid come to magical life in all their playful, passionate, savage, elemental glory. In a visually fantastic world—set in and around a pool of water—the human and the divine collide, and such familiar figures as Poseidon, King Midas and Eurydice share universal stories of love, hope, death, betrayal and transformation. Beneath clouds and rainfall, mythological characters dip in and out of the onstage pool, where the waters hold both serenity and danger. Reed Jones served as the Stage Manager for the Production.*

Reed is a fourth year, simultaneous degree candidate in Theater and Performance Studies (emphasis in Stage Management) and Business Administration at the Haas School of Business. Reed has served on the Stage Management team for several TDPS productions including Chavez Ravine, Heart of Spain, Berkeley Dance Project, Metamorphoses, *and the* Dream of Kitamura. *Outside of TDPS, Reed is the Chair of the UC Rally Committee, serves as a liaison to the office of University Development and Alumni Relations, and has had the great fortune of working with several Broadway National Tours including* Kinky Boots *(1st National),* GHOST *(1st National),* Annie *(Revival US),* Dirty Dancing *(North American),* The Sound of Music *(North American), and* Les Misérables *(North American). Reed strongly believes that the department provides students with a well-rounded education that prepares students to be the next generation of theater practitioners and scholars.*

Reed Jones
B.A. Theater and Performance Studies, 2019
B.S. Business Administration, Haas School of Business, 2019

Faculty Mentor: Laxmi Kumaran, Theater, Dance, and Performance Studies

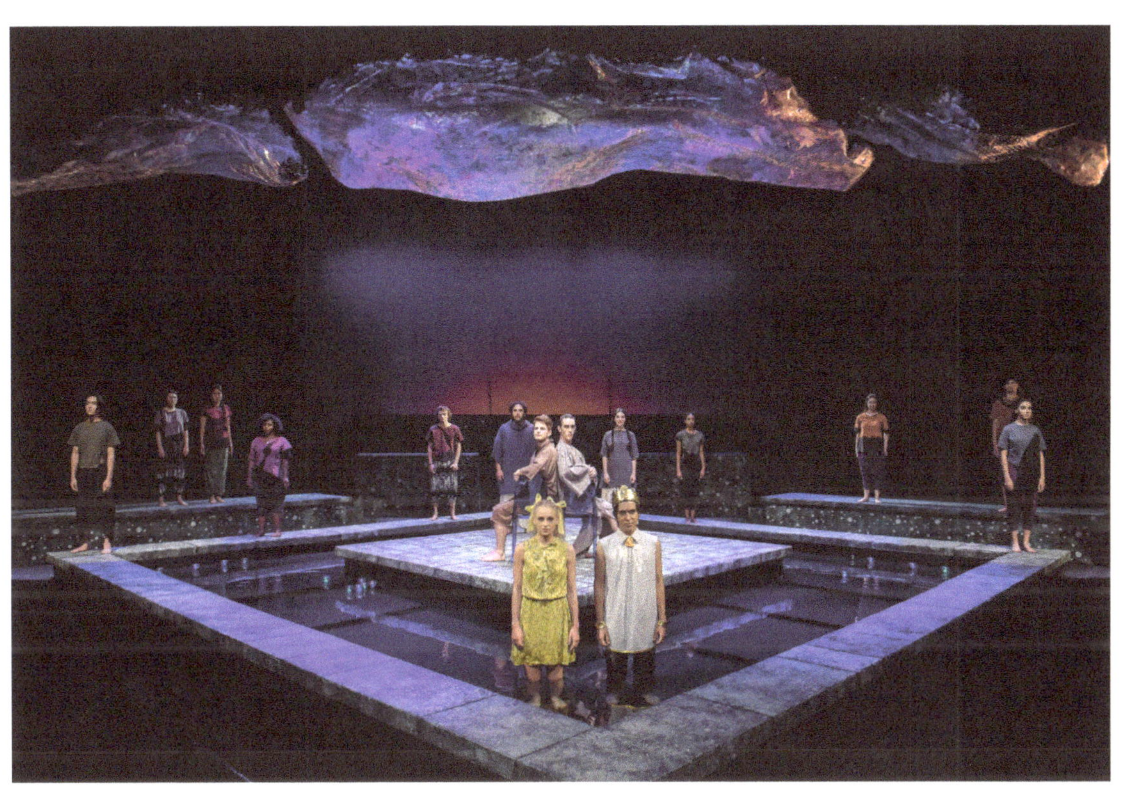

Metamorphoses, 2017. Live performance, 1 hour 25 minutes.

Yuan Zhuang

The Book from The Sky is inspired by the moon, and it incorporates Chinese elements—the specific ancient Chinese characters called "Yun Zhuan" which people can no longer understand. The work also adopts the traditional Chinese ink and wash painting method. The overall style is Zen: graceful and quiet. This work creates a sense of layer by using the translucency of the paper and controlling the amount of ink used on both the board and the paper that makes people feel distant changing without losing the whole painting's integrity. The work is to attract and block people's desire to make sense. The artist hopes that this work will prompt people to always be awed and curious about nature.

Yuan Zhuang is an artist who specializes in painting. She comes from China and now lives in the San Francisco Bay Area. She was selected as an honor student during her study of art at UC Berkeley, and was elected to the Phi Beta Kappa honor society as a lifelong member. She focuses on the emotional side of people and hopes that the beauty of human nature and the sensuous nature of art are transmitting to each other. She likes Zen and brings Zen into her works, so her works are visually light and quiet and often make people look beyond the everyday life.

Yuan Zhuang
B.A. Art Practice, 2018

Faculty Mentor: Craig Nagasawa, Art Practice

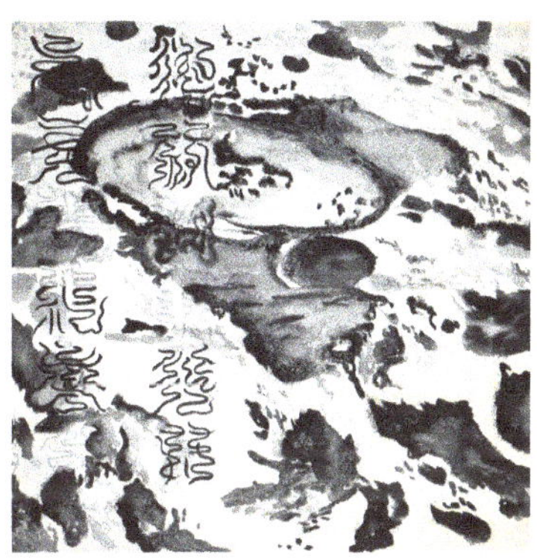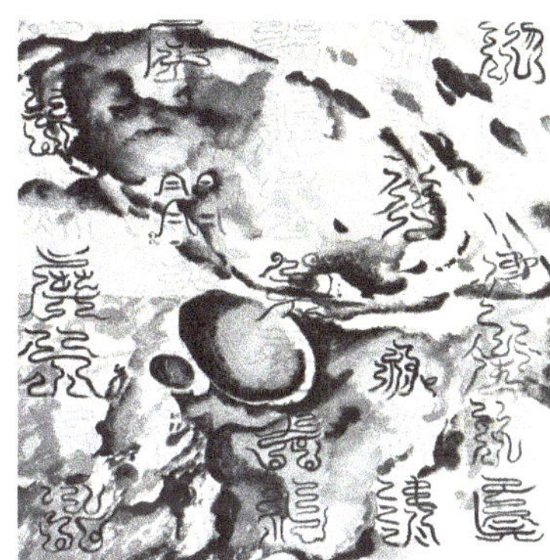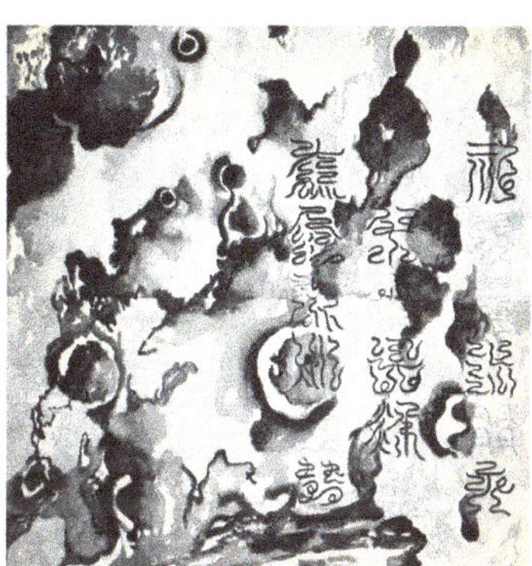

The Book From The Sky, 2018. Ink and ground pigment on handmade Japanese paper on wood board, triptych, each panel 48 x 48 in.

S.T.E.A.M.

Circuit Twister

The ultimate goal of Circuit Twister is to provide a cooperative and fun way for children to learn the concepts of basic circuitry. Modeling our design off the Hasbro game Twister, we laid out four basic circuits, or levels, on a vinyl mat in such a way as to encourage the light-hearted awkwardness the original game affords. Underneath each "gamepad" is a custom button that provides the necessary visual feedback and circuit logic to make the game functional. Through gamifying and building a sense of togetherness into an academic, and normally solitary, concept, this piece aims to both break down the seriousness intrinsic to the engineering field as well as provide a less isolating alternative to studying schematics.

Team Circuit Twister came together through the Creative Programming and Electronics (DESINV 23) course. As none of them fall into the generalized computer science or electrical engineering fields, they wanted to make a project that brought their own strengths to the table, while at the same time encompassing their own feelings on these fields as a whole.

Cade Cahalan
B.A. Product Design, 2019

Ethan Frazin
B.A. Undeclared, 2019

Chelsey Campillo
B.S. Biology, 2018

Jefrey Nacar
B.S. Chemical Engineering and Nuclear Engineering, 2018

Bennett Shaeffer
B.A. Music, 2019

Faculty Mentor: Eric Paulos, Electrical Engineering Computer Science

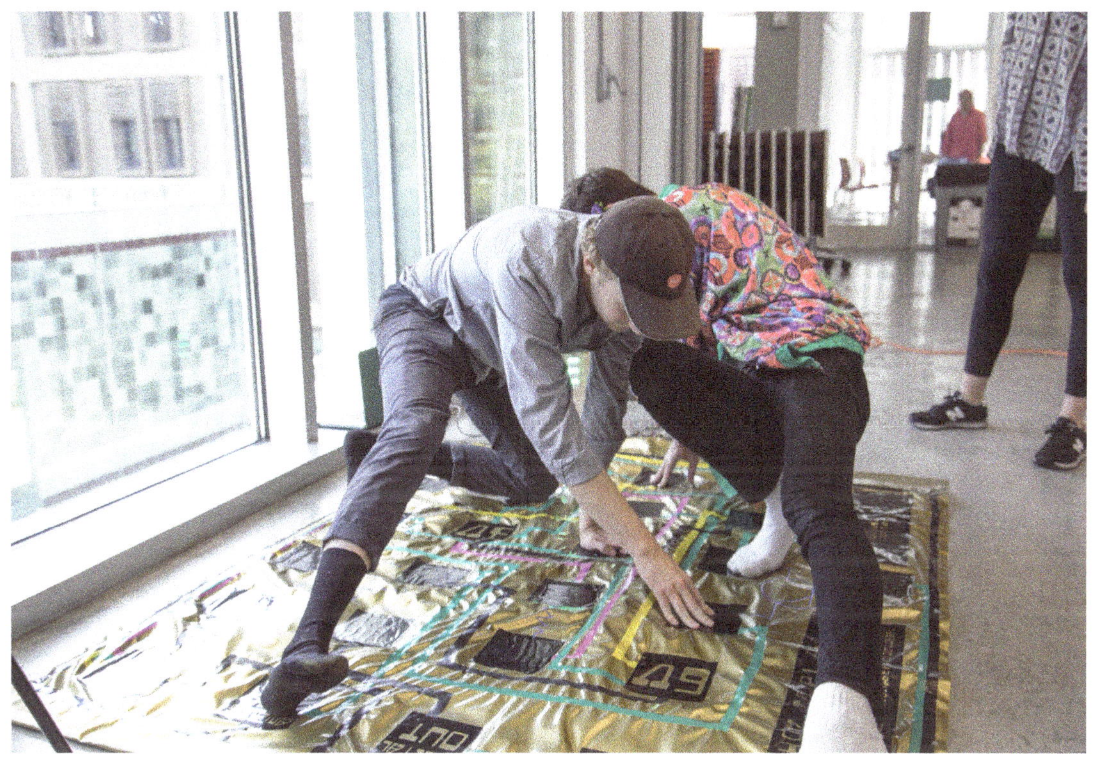

Circuit Twister, 2018. Vinyl.

Jonathan Sudano

This work is a result of Jonathan Sudano's Honors Thesis, titled "Granular and Reconstructive Synthesis Driven by Acoustic Instruments in Live Performance." The goal of the thesis was to explore the intersection of the fields of Music and Computer Science by developing novel applications of granular synthesis to live performance. The resulting instrument analyzes and utilizes input from live performance of an acoustic wind instrument, using biometric data from the performer to control and modify live audio from their instrument. In this way, the means by which the performer controls their acoustic instrument act as indirect control input for the electronic instrument. From a compositional standpoint, this presents the audience with a novel way to comprehend the physicality of wind performance.

Jonathan Sudano came to UC Berkeley with a background performing traditional jazz and a desire to write film music. He quickly discovered his love for computer science, and after deciding to major he discovered UC Berkeley CNMAT, where he took courses concerning the intersection of music and computing. Jonathan recently received the Eisner Prize in music and over the past two semesters he has had work derived from his honors thesis performed at the Center for New Music in San Francisco.

Jonathan Sudano
B.A. Music and Computer Science, 2018

Faculty Mentor: Ken Ueno, Music

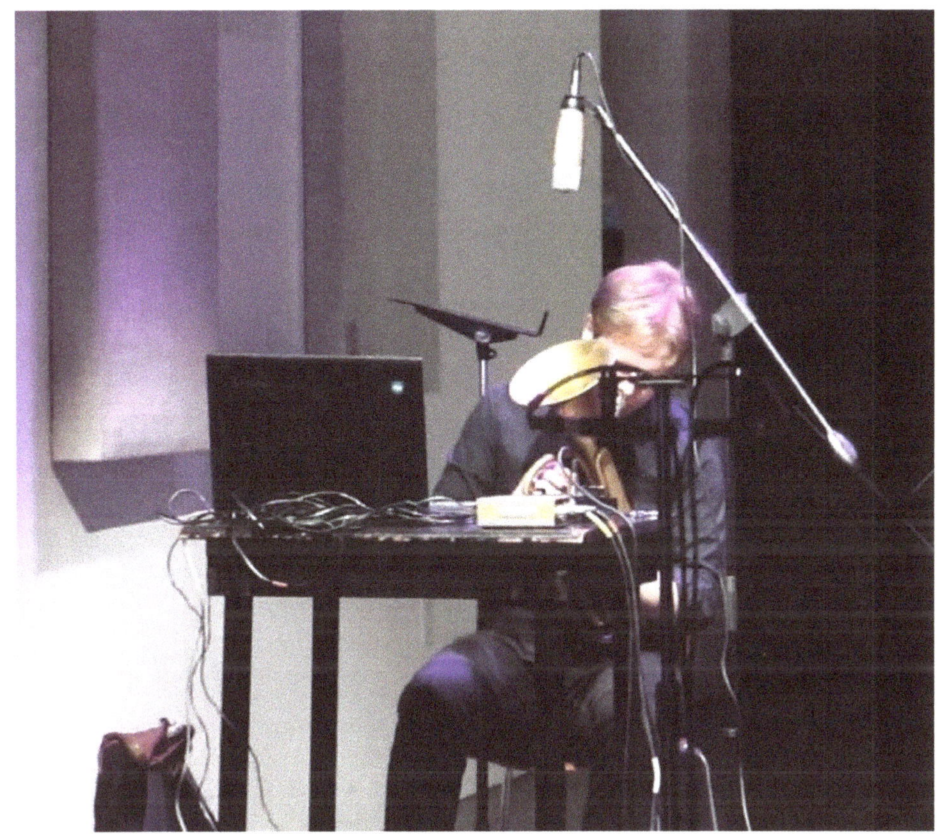

Reconstructive Granular Synthesis Engine, 2018. Electronic musical instrument in Max MSP, Variable time.

Music 158b

The students of CNMAT's advanced electronic music course "Situated Instrument Design for Musical Expression" (Music 158B) have merged together to form a collective performance group—transforming the Main Room at CNMAT into an immersive installation environment. Students merge spatialized sound with body tracking, interactive lighting, projection mapping and animations. Audience members will at once control and experience a nuanced field of expression where their movement affects their surroundings in exciting ways.

The group consists of undergraduate students of CNMAT's advanced electronic music course "Situated Instrument Design for Musical Expression." Each member of the group brought unique skill sets from their respective background, ranging from computer science, music theory, visual art, and cognitive science. The group was trained in developing in the Max/MSP environment, which was complemented with CNMAT technologies.

Ryan Hayes
B.S. Electrical Engineering
and Computer Science, 2019

Rocky Lubbers
B.A. Cognitive Science, 2020

Gregory Oliva
B.S. Electrical Engineering
and Computer Science, 2019

Ray Savord
B.A. German and Music, 2020

William Sheu
B.A. Computer Science, 2019

Trevor Van de Velde
B.A. Undeclared, 2020

Ben Vu
B.A. Undeclared, 2020

Faculty Mentor: David Coll, Music

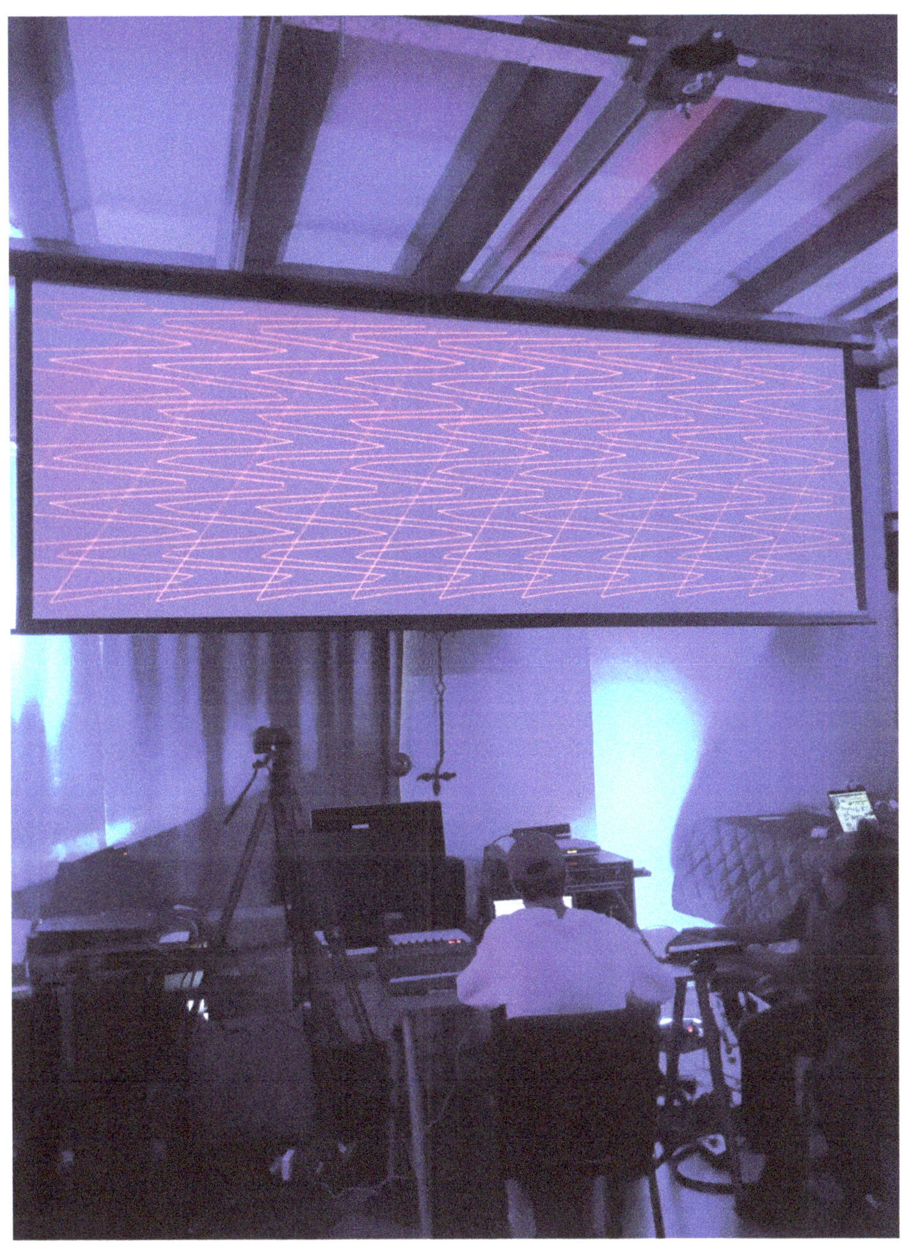

Music 158b Interactive Installation, April 26, 2018. Interactive installation in CNMAT's main room. Consists of hung wooden panels, a projection screen, an xbox kinect, led/halogen lights, computers running Max/MSP, and speakers, 2 hours.

Social Butterfly

Social Butterfly encourages activity-based socialization amongst children using wings as a medium, capturing the playfulness, confidence, and larger-than-life personality associated with wearing wings. The wearer can attract the attention of nearby playmates by triggering a motor-actuated fluttering motion. Our wings also celebrate creativity and foster conversation – children can draw and write on six panels to create a set of visual, personalized conversation topics. Playmates can touch a fragment of the wing mosaic, which illuminates a panel as a conversation starter.

Social Butterfly was the collaborative effort of Justine Chia, Vivian Liu, Varna Vasudevan, and Yuki Zhan. Its creation was guided by the expertise of Invention Lab managers and supervisors Chris Myers, Kuan-Ju Wu, and Mitchell Karchemsky. Justine is a neurobiologist who loves exploring and creating at the intersection of art and science. Vivian is an undergraduate who enjoys pulling 2D into 3D through creative computing. Varna is an undergraduate interested in creating delightful user experiences through physical and digital product design. Yuki is a masters student delighted in engineering beautiful and functional things.

Justine Chia
Ph.D. Molecular & Cell Biology, 2019

Varna Vasudevan
B.S. Mechanical Engineering, 2019

Vivian Liu
B.A. Cognitive Science and Computer
Science, 2019

Yuki Zhan
M.S. Mechanical Engineering, 2018

Faculty Mentor: Eric Paulos, Electrical Engineering Computer Science

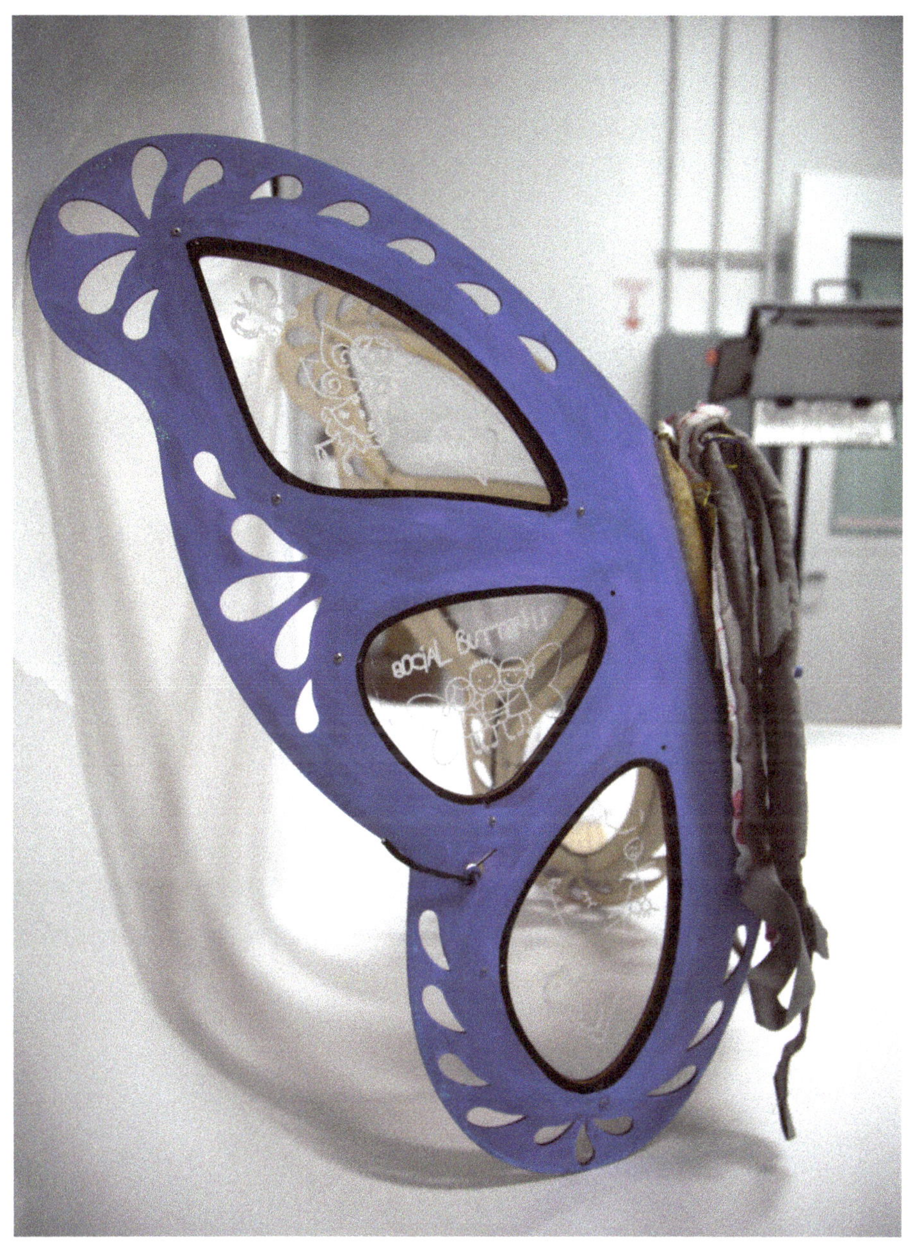

Social Butterfly, 2018. Laser-cut wood, acrylic, electronics, 50 x 5 x 30 in.

A+D PROJECTS

ARTS PASSPORT MOBILE APP
DANCING BRIDGES

Arts Passport Mobile App

The Arts Access and Engagement App was formed as a collaboration between the UC Berkeley Fung Institute for Engineering Leadership and the Arts + Design Initiative. It weaves together campus communities and provides financial accessibility to the arts. Under the guidance of the campus's Chief Technology Officer and Arts + Design staff, a team of five graduate students built a dynamic, integrated, and interactive platform that exists on the new Campus App. Students, teachers, curators, audiences, and Bay Area arts organizations can use the app to learn from each other and actively participate in arts events.

Kyra Chang
M.Eng. Civil Engineering, 2018

Raina Pan
M.Eng. Industrial Engineering and
Operations Research, 2018

Luna Izpisua Rodriguez
M.Eng. Industrial Engineering and
Operations Research, 2018

Alexandre Vincent
MEng Industrial Engineering and
Operations Research, 2018

Jasmine Zhou
M.Eng. Industrial Engineering and Operations Research, 2018

Faculty Mentor: William Allison, Chief Technology Officer; Wayne Lee Delker, Executive Director, Fung Institute for Engineering Leadership; Sarah Fullerton, Communications Manager, Berkeley Arts + Design; Nicholas Matthews, Department of Music

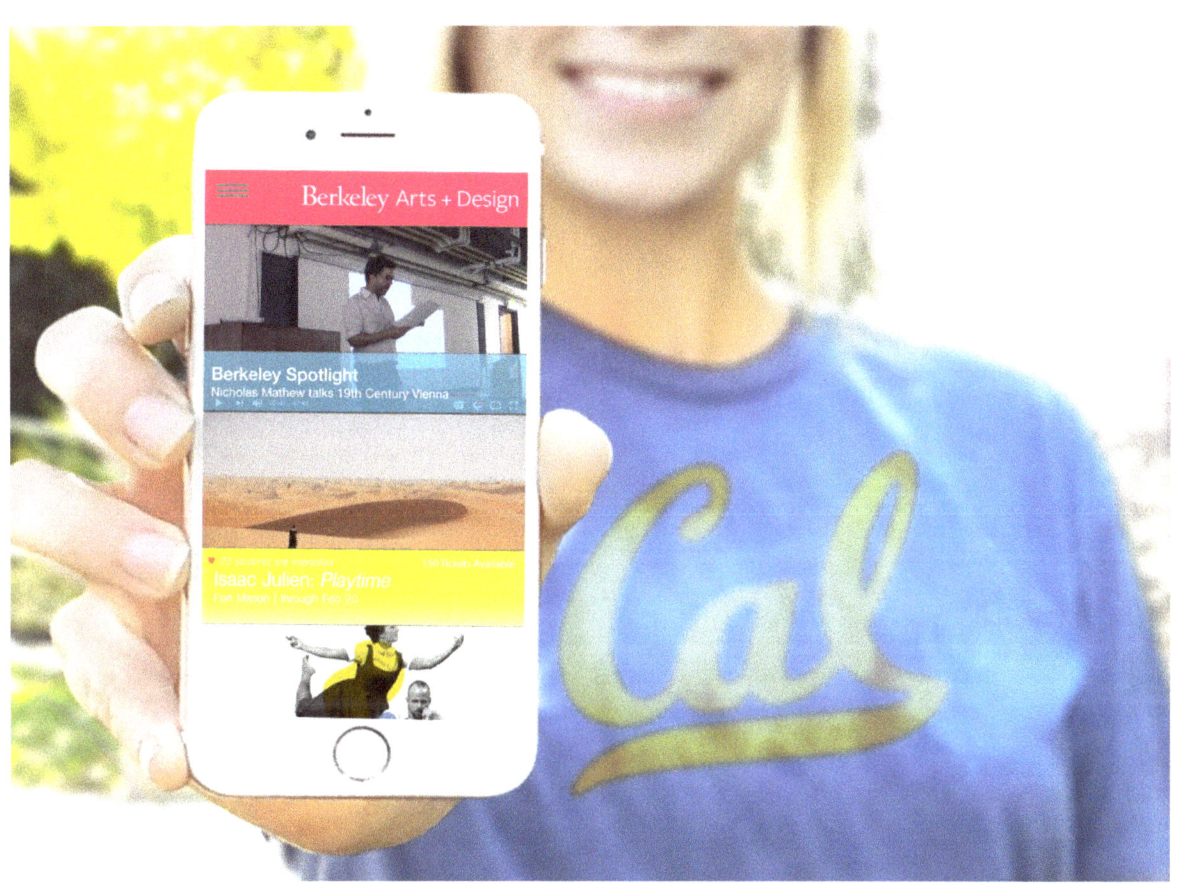

UC Berkeley Arts Access App, 2017 - Present. Digital, iOS and Android.

Dancing Bridges

Dancing Bridges is a landscape architectural response to the Dwinelle Annex and its courtyard—the home, hearth, and launch pad for Berkeley's Arts + Design Initiative. Professor Walter Hood asked teams of students to re-imagine the courtyard as a space that embodied the creative goals of A+D and public heritage of UC-Berkeley. In a studio course inspired by David Hockney's collage concept of "joiners" as well as the graphic and choreographic potential of "notational systems," this student found in "capoeira" an apt metaphor for re-imagining a landscape and a hardscape in motion. While the six sides of the courtyard served as their basic spatial envelope, Dancing Bridges pushed beyond the envelope to plot walkways and 'dancing bridges' across Strawberry Creek, re-orienting this backstage space as a front stage proscenium with new paths of travel. Recalling the history of Craftsman campus architecture in this small building designed by John Galen Howard—Berkeley's first campus architect—Dancing Bridges links Berkeley's past architectural heritage to its future creative aspirations. In visualizations, narratives, and notations, it offers new kind of spatial dancing on a campus where many have danced before.

Dancing Bridges is a Case Study by Alexander Broad for Professor Walter Hood's class, LD ARCH 200B Case Studies in Landscape Design. Group project and other case studies by Molly Butcher, Jessica Colvin, Felix De Rosen, Sarah Fitzgerald, Meghan Kanady, Julia Prince, and Logan Woodruff.

Faculty Mentor: Walter Hood, Landscape and Environmental Design

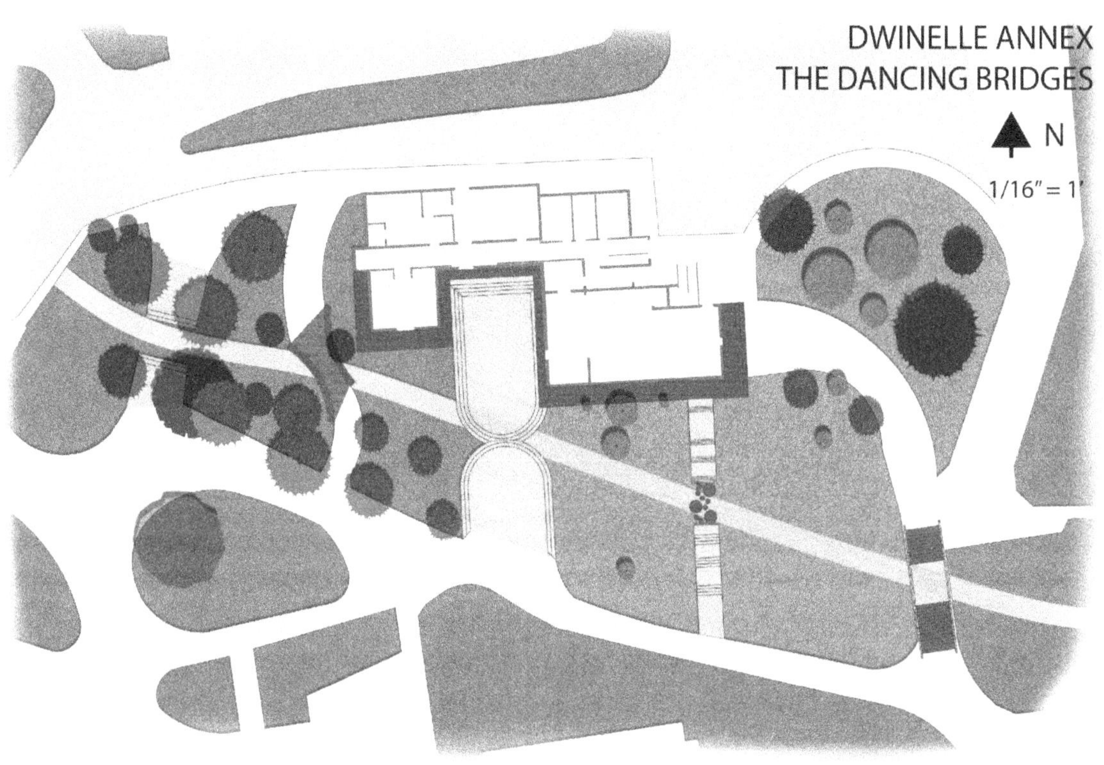

Landscape Design Case Studies, 2018. [Images 1, 2, and 3 by Alexander Broad. Images 4 and 5 group projects.]

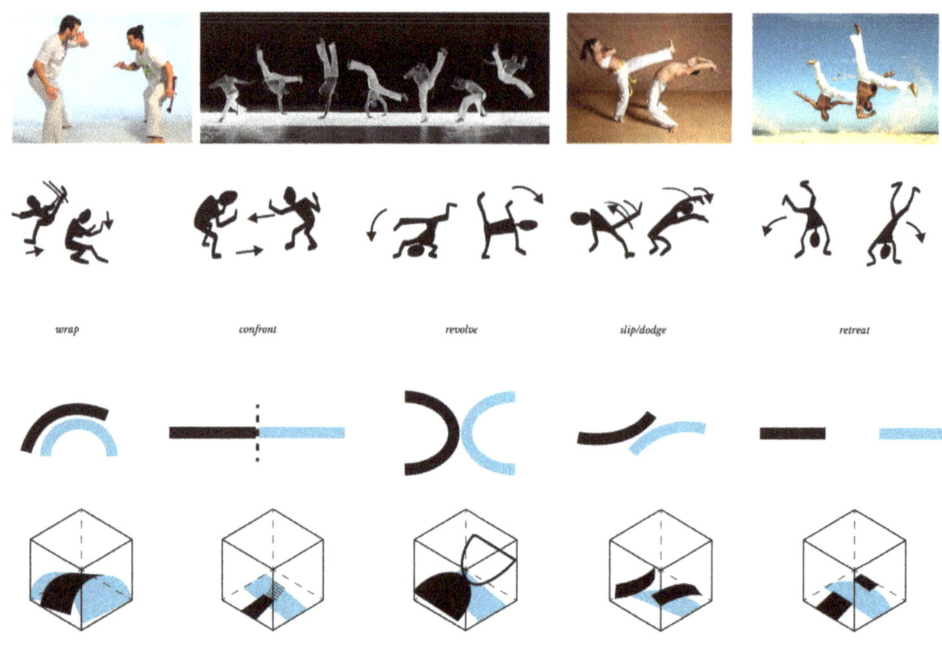

wrap
confront
revolve
slip/dodge
retreat

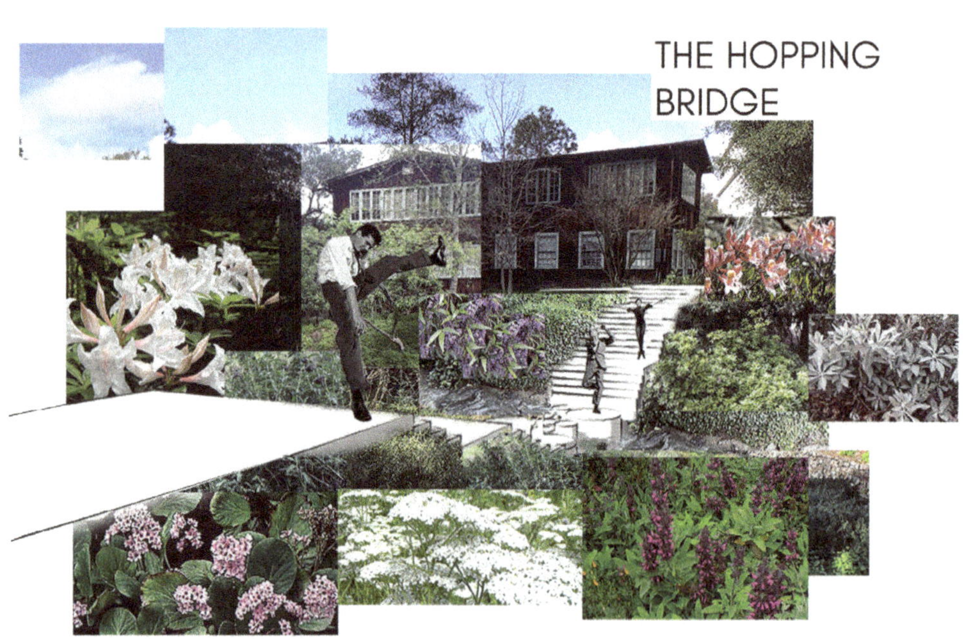

THE HOPPING
BRIDGE

COURTYARD

TOPOGRAPHY

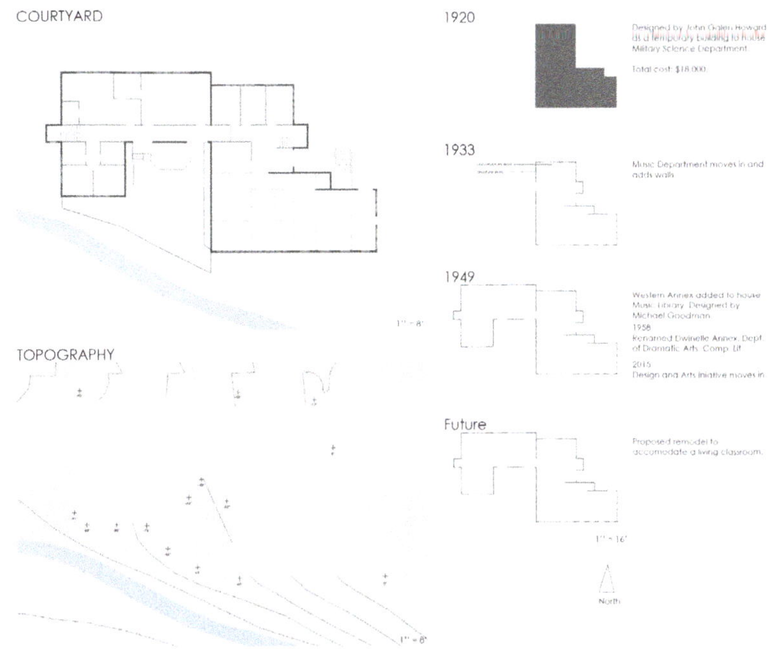

Site Circulation
1st Floor

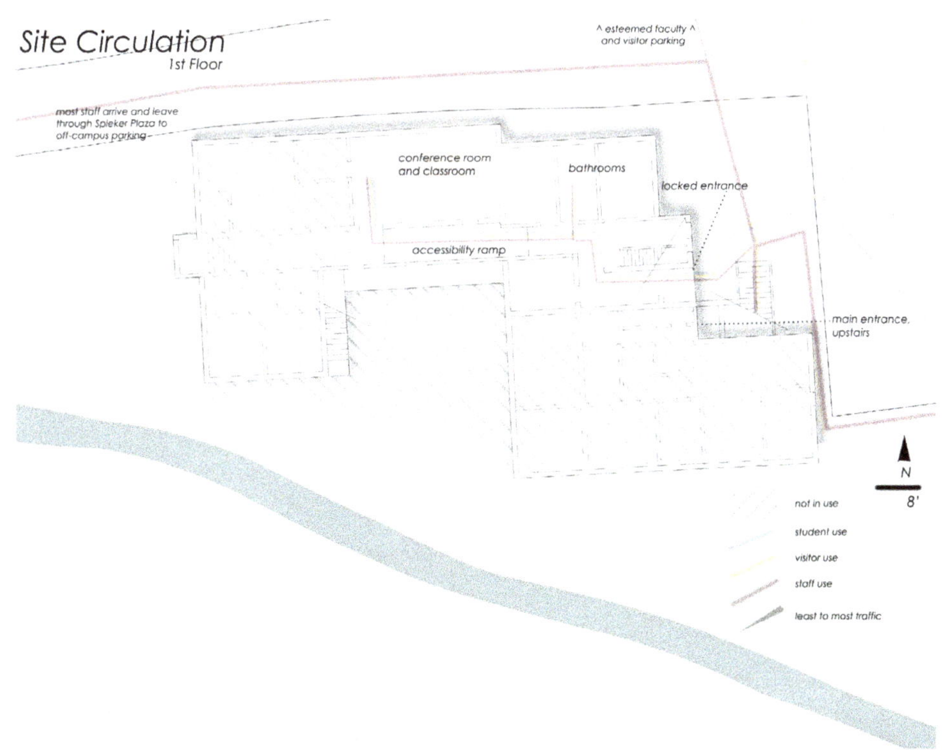

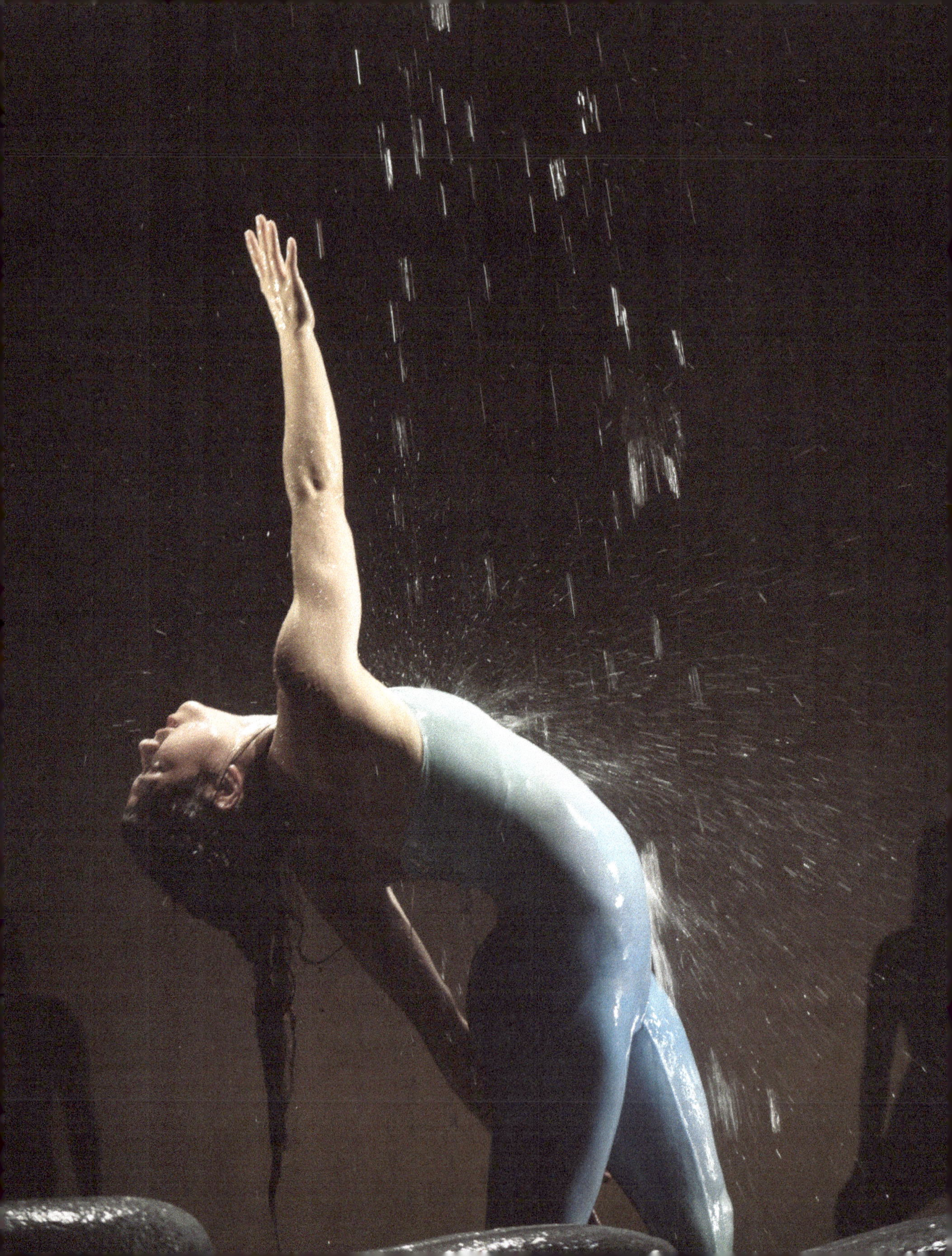

AESTHETICS

CITIES

Siteworks Team: Aniston-Maylee Breslin, B.A. Art History, 2018; Helen Jiang, B.A. Film and Media Studies, 2018; Amy Loo, B.A. Political Science, 2018; Tiffany Meng, B.A. Urban Studies, 2019; Ricky Montali, B.A. Art Practice, 2018; Kathleen O'Connor, B.A. Theater, Dance and Performance Studies, 2018; Patricia Midy, B.A. Individual Major, Space and Character, 2019; Moira Peckham, B.A. Anthropology and Archaeology, 2018; Michael Qi, B.A. Undeclared, 2021; Peihan Qian, B.A. Architecture, 2020; Hannah Ricker, B.A. Development Studies, 2018; Natalia Rico, B.S. Conservation and Resource Studies, 2019; Briana Salmon, B.A. Architecture, 2018; Daniel Sanchez, B.A. Architecture, 2018; Grace Treffinger, B.S. Conservation and Resource Studies, 2018. Faculty Mentors: Ghigo DiTommaso, Landscape Architecture and Environmental Planning; Erica Chong Shuch, Theater, Dance & Performance Studies; Susan Moffat, City and Regional Planning, Global Urban Humanities Initiative. Graduate Student Mentor: Annie Danis, Archaeology/ Anthropology.

ENVIRONMENT

Alvaro Azcárraga, B.A. Art Practice and Molecular & Cell Biology, 2018. Faculty Mentor: Brody Reiman, Art Practice; Stephanie Syjuco, Art Practice.

Fantastick Team: Arnaud Bard de Coutance, M.Eng, 2018; Lieyah Dagan, B.A. Interdisciplinary Studies, 2018; Silvia Kim, B.A. Cognitive Science, 2018; Alyssa Li, MIMS, 2019. Faculty Mentor: Eric Paulos, Electrical Engineering Computer Science; Christine Dierk.

Flipper Filter Team: Tia LaMore , B.S. Integrative Biology, 2020; Reem Makkawi, B.A. Architecture, 2018. Faculty Mentor: Robert J. Full, Integrative Biology.

FABRICATION

Alexandra Grabow, B.A. Art Practice and Theater and Performance Studies, 2020. Faculty Mentor: Annie Smart, Theater, Dance, and Performance Studies.

Cantilevered Stairs Team: Chutikarn Cholsaipan, B.A. Architecture, 2019; Viet Nguyen, B.A. Architecture, 2019; Jacqueline Serrano, B.A. Architecture, 2019; Camille Vistica, B.A. Architecture, 2019. Faculty Mentor: Jamay Li.

Concrete Puzzle Team: Setareh Barimani, B.A. Architecture, 2018; Natya Dharmosetio, B.A. Architecture, 2018. Faculty Mentor: Jordan Cayanan, Architecture.

Kickstarter Team: Arianna Ninh, B.A. Cognitive Science, 2019; Varna Vasudevan, B.S. Mechanical Engineering, 2019; Essie Xu, B.A. Economics, 2019. Faculty Mentor: Eric Paulos, Electrical Engineering Computer Science.

Le Stair Team: Brenda Delgado-Barajas , B.A. Architecture, 2018; David Musa, B.A. Architecture, 2018; Elizabeth Romo, B.A. Architecture, 2018; Jonathan Solis, B.A. Architecture, 2018. Faculty Mentor: Dana Buntrock, Architecture; David Jaehning, Architecture; Jeremy Ferguson, Architecture.

Morphosis Team: Benzi Blatman, B.A. Landscape Architecture, 2020; Lana Dementsova, B.A. Architecture, 2019; Cody Lambrecht, B.A. Architecture, 2019; Natasha Landicho, B.A. Urban Studies, 2020. Faculty Mentor: Dana Buntrock, Architecture.

Polygonal Fireplace Team: Josselenn Maldonado , B.A. Architecture, 2020; Rui Wang, CED-GAP, 2020 ; Delphina Wedell, B.A. Architecture, 2020. Faculty Mentor: Dana Buntrock, Architecture; Nikita Tugarin, Architecture.

The Wood Planter Project Team: Setareh Barimani, B.A. Architecture, 2018; Natya Dharmosetio, B.A. Architecture, 2018; Ernie Theurer, B.A. Architecture, 2018. Faculty Mentor: Jordan Cayanan, Architecture.

Yohana Ansari-Thomas, B.A. Spatial Performance & Design, 2019. Faculty Mentor: Annie Smart, Theater, Dance, and Performance Studies.

GENDER + SEXUALITY

Bank of Hysteria Team: Malika Imhotep, Ph.D. African Diaspora Studies; Jessica Liu, B.A. Cognitive Science and Asian American/Asian Diaspora Studies, 2019; Becca Milman, B.A. Computer Science, 2017; Frances Thai, B.A. Computer Science, 2017; Phyllis Thai, B.A. Interdisciplinary Studies, 2018. Faculty Mentor: Jill Miller, Berkeley Center for New Media.

Eyeris Team: Silvia Kim, B.A. Cognitive Science, 2019; George Moore, Ph.D. Mechanical Engineering, 2021; Arianna Ninh, B.A. Cognitive Science, 2019; Katherine Qiu, B.A. Individual Major, 2019. Faculty Mentor: Eric Paulos, Electrical Engineering Computer Science.

Hari Lee, B.A. Social Welfare, 2019. Faculty Mentor: Lise Gaston, English.

Madeleine Curtis, B.S. Neurobiology, 2021. Faculty Mentor: Lise Gaston, English.

Narges Poursadeqi, B.A. Art Practice, 2018. Faculty Mentor: Brody Reiman, Art Practice.

Sanaz Khosravi, B.A. Art Practice, 2018. Faculty Mentor: Azin Seraj, Art Practice.

GLOBAL CULTURES

Amanda Kachadoorian, B.A. Art Practice. Faculty Mentor: Brody Reiman, Art Practice.

Deconstructing Walls Team: Purva Juvekar, M.Eng. Mechanical Engineering, 2018; Crystal Lee, B.A. Cognitive Science, 2018; Edward Rivero, LLC Ph.D.; Sally Tran, B.A. Cognitive Science, 2018. Faculty Mentor: Eric Paulos, Electrical Engineering Computer Science; Chris Meyers, Citris and the Banatao Institute.

Livia Gomes Demarchi, B.A. Theater and Performance Studies, 2018. Faculty Mentor: Angela Marino, Theater, Dance, and Performance Studies.

Patrick McBurnie, B.A. English, 2018. Faculty Mentor: Lyn Hejinian, English; Robert Hass, English.

Sanaz Khosravi, B.A. Art Practice, 2018. Faculty Mentor: Allan deSouza, Art Practice.

Sergio Mendez-Torres, B.A. English, 2018. Faculty Mentor: Lyn Hejinian, English.

HEALTH

Artists in Residents Team: Kyle Gibson, B.A. Public Health, 2019; Mark Houdi, B.A. Molecular & Cell Biology, 2019; Krupa Modi, B.A. Public Health, 2019; Monica Schreiber, B.A. Public Health, 2019; Rasika Sudharshan, B.A. Cognitive Science and Molecular & Cell Biology, 2019; Allie Yip, B.A. Integrative Biology, 2019. Faculty Mentor: Phillip Denny, Big Ideas Team.

Bonafide Team: Daniel Chang, B.A. Economics, 2018; Ji Soo Kim, B.A. Cognitive Science, 2018; Sarah Malone, B.A. Cognitive Science, 2020; Ivy Nguyen, B.A. Computer Science, 2020; Priyanka Saiprasad, B.A. Cognitive Science and Data Science, 2020. Faculty Mentor: James Pierce, School of Information; Claire Dunnington, Haas School of Business.

Hazanne (Sidney) Likwong, B.A. Art Practice and Urban Studies, 2019. Faculty Mentor: Maggie Lawson, Art Practice.

PerSpectacles Team: Nour Eldifrawy, B.S. Materials Science and Engineering, 2018; Leeann Hu, B.A. Molecular & Cell Biology, 2019; Crystal Lee, B.A. Cognitive Science, 2018; Nigel Mevana, B.S. Mechanical Engineering, 2018. Faculty Mentor: Eric Paulos, Electrical Engineering Computer Science.

Rae Maxwell-Ross, B.A. Art Practice, 2018. Faculty Mentor: Brody Reiman, Art Practice.

Smart Can Team: Fiona Duerr, B.A. Urban Studies, 2018; Nour Eldien Eldifrawy, B.S. Materials Science & Engineering, 2018; Purva Juvekar, M.Eng. Mechanical Engineering, 2018; Christina Pappas, MBA, 2018. Faculty Mentor: Eric Paulos, Electrical Engineering Computer Science.

Tearrarium Team: Lieyah Dagan, B.A. Design for Urban Life, 2018; Fiona Duerr, B.A. Urban Studies, 2018; Seiyoung Jang, M.F.A. Electronic Music & Recording Media, Mills College Department of Music, 2018; Crystal Lee, B.A. Cognitive Science, 2018; Arianna Ninh, B.A. Cognitive Science, 2019. Faculty Mentor: Jill Miller, Berkeley Center for New Media.

Universal Socket Prosthetic Team: Dominic Chiavacci, B.S. Bioengineering, 2018; Hunter Garnier, B.S. Mechanical Engineering, 2018; Akhilesh Mishra, B.S. Mechanical Engineering, 2018; Stephen Shelnut, B.S. Civil Engineering, 2019. Faculty Mentor: Grace O'Connell, Mechanical Engineering.

SPIRITUALITY

Melissa Chapman, B.A. Theater and Performance Studies; Minor in Dance and Performance Studies. Faculty Mentor: James Graham, Theater, Dance, and Performance Studies.

Reed Jones, B.A. Theater and Performance Studies, 2019, and B.S. Business Administration, 2019. Faculty Mentor: Laxmi Kumaran, Theater, Dance, and Performance Studies.

Yuan Zhuang, B.A. Art Practice, 2018. Faculty Mentor: Craig Nagasawa, Art Practice.

S.T.E.A.M.

Circuit Twister Team: Cade Cahalan, B.A. Product Design, 2019; Chelsey Campillo, B.S. Biology, 2018; Ethan Frazin, B.A. Undeclared, 2019; Jefrey Nacar, B.S. Chemical Engineering and Nuclear Engineering, 2018; Bennett Shaeffer, B.A. Music, 2019. Faculty Mentor: J.D. Zamfirescu-Pereira.

Jonathan Sudano, B.A. Music and Computer Science, 2018. Faculty Mentor: Ken Ueno, Music.

Music 158b Team: Ryan Hayes, B.S. Electrical Engineering and Computer Science, 2019; Rocky Lubbers, B.A. Cognitive Science, 2020; Gregory Oliva, B.S. Electrical Engineering and Computer Science, 2019; Ray Savord, B.A. German and Music, 2020; William Sheu, B.A. Computer Science, 2019; Trevor Van de Velde, B.A. Undeclared, 2020; Ben Vu, B.A. Undeclared, 2020. Faculty Mentor: David Coll, Music.

Social Butterfly Team: Justine Chia, Ph.D. Molecular & Cell Biology, 2019; Vivian Liu, B.A. Cognitive Science and Computer Science, 2019; Varna Vasudevan, B.S. Mechanical Engineering, 2019; Yuki Zhan, M.S. Mechanical Engineering, 2018. Faculty Mentor: Eric Paulos, Electrical Engineering Computer Science.

A+D PROJECTS

Arts Access App Team: Kyra Chang, M.Eng. Civil Engineering, 2018; Raina Pan, M.Eng. Industrial Engineering and Operations Research, 2018; Luna Izpisua Rodriguez, M.Eng. Industrial Engineering and Operations Research, 2018; Alexandre Vincent, MEng Industrial Engineering and Operations Research, 2018; Jasmine Zhou, M.Eng. Industrial Engineering and Operations Research, 2018. Faculty Mentor: William Allison, Chief Technology Officer; Wayne Lee Delker, Executive Director, Fung Institute for Engineering Leadership; Sarah Fullerton, Communications Manager, Berkeley Arts + Design; Nicholas Matthews, Department of Music.

Landscape Design Team: Alexander Broad, Molly Butcher, Jessica Colvin, Felix De Rosen, Sarah Fitzgerald, Meghan Kanady, Julia Prince, and Logan Woodruff. Faculty Mentor: Walter Hood, Landscape and Environmental Design.

With special thanks to Paris Cotz, Amber Fogarty, Sarah Fullerton Kolker, Les Gorske, Luna Izpisua-Rodriguez, Massimo Pacchione, Lauren Pearson, Soomin Suh, and all the students and faculty who made this beautiful compilation possible.

Berkeley Arts + Design

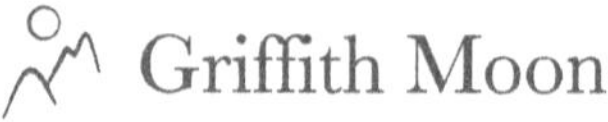

Griffith Moon